FRANCOPHONE MIGRATIONS, FRENCH ISLAM AND WELLBEING

FRANCOPHONE MIGRATIONS, FRENCH ISLAM AND WELLBEING
The Soninké Foyer in Paris

Dafne Accoroni

berghahn
NEW YORK · OXFORD
www.berghahnbooks.com

First published in 2022 by
Berghahn Books
www.berghahnbooks.com

Library of Congress Cataloging-in-Publication Data

A C.I.P. cataloging record is available from the Library of Congress
Library of Congress Cataloging in Publication Control Number: 2022017373

British Library Cataloguing in Publication Data

A catalogue record for this book is available from the British Library.

ISBN 978-1-80073-627-6 hardback
ISBN 978-1-80073-628-3 ebook

https://doi.org/10.3167/9781800736276

To Silvia and Agustin, my heart

Armando and Carla, my parents

Twins and family never die, much like myths and love

CONTENTS

ILLUSTRATIONS

Figures

Tables

ACKNOWLEDGEMENTS

I would like to thank Prof. Roland Littlewood, Prof. Michael Rowlands and Dr Maurice Lipsedge for their inspiration, teaching, example and support, which led to the conclusion of my work. They enabled me to face with determination and courage the difficulties involved in my research, focused on Islam and the Muslim community at a moment in which they are encountering, probably more than ever, the negative biases provoked by radical Islam and terrorism. The former's encyclopaedic knowledge and guidance has been invaluable in this endeavour.

I am also grateful to the Marie Curie Prestige Funding that allowed me to pursue further my analysis of sub-Saharan migrations to Europe at Université Jean Moulin Lyon3, Lyon, France. Here, I could bring to the fore an unprecedented line of research by introducing the geopolitical dimension of *francophonie* that characterises these migrations and particularly Islam. 'French' Islam has become a pressing issue in France, where a heated debate has been shaped by the colours of the Republic versus what are perceived to be communitarian drifts, all the while giving way to a serious institutionalisation of Muslim representative bodies and to the training of imams.

Furthermore, my grateful acknowledgement goes to the people of Foyer93. Initially suspicious of me, they have become over time affectionate respondents and friends. First of all, I thank the imam, who granted me access to the life of Foyer93 after the residents' delegate had given his permission; and the barman who allowed me to spend time at the cafeteria, where I had more chances to meet people and observe their dynamics. In the end, I was honoured as a special guest, invited to have lunch at the canteen and given free tea and coffee. On my leaving day, the workers at the forge produced a pair of earrings, which they made especially for me. My experience at Foyer93 will stay with me forever, as will those earrings, its concrete sign.

There are many people and organizations in academia and in the field, who have variously contributed to my work: my appreciation goes to them too. Among these are the associations either working for or run by migrants with which I could side and from whom I could learn, hands-on. They facilitated my way into the field. I am eternally beholden to them.

Finally, my thoughts go to my family, without whom my research would not even have started. They have relentlessly helped me through the highs and lows of this intellectual and emotional endeavour. In particular, Silvia, my twin sister, who is no longer with us today, has been my constant point of reference. I giggle at the realisation that my sister and I have solved in a flash the centuries-long medieval dispute over the ontological reality of God. What has once become cannot but be forever.

Introduction

Looking for Islam in Paris, Finding a *Foyer*

I carried out my anthropological investigation among members of the Soninké[1] migrant community, from Kayes, Mali, living in a *foyer* (henceforth Foyer93) in Paris between June 2005 and September 2006, and then on several short fieldwork trips since then.[2] I chose the *foyers* as a vantage point of observation because they are a central issue for the French Republic historically, politically and socially. Any research on Muslim migrants in Paris will sooner or later lead to the *foyers*, where first-generation migrants live. Scattered around Paris and the Île-de-France region, the *foyers* exemplify the plight of Muslim migrants and with it, the tangible construction of vulnerability, exclusion and difference. France is the country that attracts the majority of the Francophone West African migration to Europe, both from rural areas and urban centres, and particularly from the Senegal River Valley, cutting across Senegal, Mauritania and Mali. It is estimated that '400,000 migrants from sub-Saharan Africa reside in France; between 1990 and 1999 the percentage of Malians has increased by 21.2%, and the Senegalese population by 28.3%' (Sargent et al. 2009: 6). Part of the influx has been due to the family reunification policy issued in 1975, after the restriction of labour migration. This led to 'a process of feminization of migration from West African countries and the appearance of second-generation West Africans born in France' (Trauner 2005:228). With the tightening of the family reunification rules through the Pasqua Law – named after the minister who issued it in 1993 – and with a surplus of manpower in the economy, migration became less structural to the French economy, and circular migration increasingly difficult to carry out. The process made become those who once had the right to residence in France – either thanks to the principle of *jus soli* or because they had obtained legal status –undocumented people, *sans-papiers*. It appears in fact that between 1997 and 1998, 41 per cent of Malians and 29 per cent of Senegalese people applying for regularisation already had documents allowing them to reside in France (Lessault et al. 2009). Illegal migration might indeed be seen as a temporary status in the process of regularisation: this was the case for 31 per cent of the migrants who obtained legal status in the period 1999–2006. Overall, sub-Saharan migration only represents 12 per cent of inward migration to France, and the section of the male migrant population that my work addresses, amounts to about one hundred and fifty thousand men, spread across seven hundred *foyers*, of which 250 are situated in the Île-de-France region (op. cit.: 224).

The first *foyers* emerged as a consequence of the reconstruction of France, which was in need of a labour force in the aftermath of the Second World War. The first residents were Algerians. At the time, these buildings resembled military areas under the control of a guard who watched over them permanently. The *foyers* now have a completely different status: the migrants are residents with whom neither the mayor of Paris, the police or other social figures can interfere, unless criminal activities take place. Given the number of illegal migrants present at Foyer93, one wonders in fact how this can be. Because of the infamous uprisings of the 1970s, in which hundreds of Algerians were killed in a strike[3] (Fall 2005), and thanks to the ongoing work of social services and associations in the *foyers*, the latter have reached the status of *parc social*, or social housing, granting their residents the right to their privacy.[4] Nevertheless, the *foyers* are still no-go areas for ordinary French people. Those in Paris are particularly unsightly, because they are the oldest and have never been restored: many are falling apart and security and health are never guaranteed there. Open sewage, no anti-fire measures, no hygiene in the collective kitchens and other such issues make one wonder whether Islam is really the core problem. Clearly, the entanglement of political and economic interests with the social reality of how West African migrants live in France entails an (anthropological) understanding of the issues surrounding the phenomenon. French ideas of the individual, citizenship and secularism collide with the way that the Soninké migrants understand how to participate in society as Muslims in a meaningful way.

The choice of Foyer93 as my fieldwork site is not casual: this *foyer* is one of those that are known as *foyers-taudis*, or slums. These were part of the post-war housing project aimed at transforming ex-factories into large dormitories for the migrant labour force. At the time, these were seen as temporary. Like Foyer93, other *foyers-taudis* are also organised ethnically. They reopen, or rather perpetuate, the debate about the integration of new citizens of migrant descent in France and the cultural adjustments necessary to make this happen. The Soninkés in Paris are now into their third generation, and yet migration from Kayes continues through trajectories similar to those described twenty years ago by anthropologists, with the *foyers*, where people cram together with their few belongings in small rooms, still at the centre of the process. These *foyers* have survived without much having been done to improve them. The physical space that the residents inhabit determines inextricably their subjectivity: the rooms do not allow anyone the peace of mind to sleep at night, let alone any privacy. The common areas, such as the canteen and the cafeteria, provide the residents with a space in which to relax, yet other boundaries intervene to make even those areas disciplined: caste divisions, age groups and seniority in migration create and recreate space and priorities continuously. The well-being of the residents resonates with and is strictly linked to the materiality of Foyer93. The ageing of the residents, along with that of the building, demonstrates the trap into which they have fallen: their expected temporary stay in France has become a life-long stay; their illegal status has in some cases never been cleared; they have lived in France as invisible people, while being absent from their homeland. They are neither here nor there, neither citizens nor migrants. As defined by Sayad (1998), the latter are people whose mobility is constitutive of their condition. Foyer93 defies this understanding as much as it tempts one into functionalist ideas of a pathological body politic, which nonetheless ignore 'questions of social change, oppression and unequal power' (Littlewood 1991: 697).

Notwithstanding the small number of people living there in comparison to the wider migrant population, the *foyers* are the gateway to future housing and work for the migrants (Timera 1996), especially when they are illegal. In this way, the *foyers* are representative of these migrants' strategies for settling in the big city, since they have hosted, and still host, different ethnic groups from the Sahel. They are organised by village of origin – thus resulting in ethnic patterns, in Paris as much as in other towns of France, such as Marseille and Lyon. France is now the second destination of the overall West African migration trends after the USA, while Southern European countries such as Spain, Italy and Portugal have emerged first as alternative destinations and in recent years as transition countries (Wihtol de Wenden 2016; Mohammedi 2014; Belguidoum et al. 2015; Saraiva 2008). Nonetheless, African migration towards OECD countries is lower than to the Global South[5], in line with the current international trend determined by South–South migrations[6]. So, what is really at stake when European countries vow to 'tackle migration'?

The stink, dirt, insecurity and noise of Foyer93 tell us upon entering what the residents face daily: exclusion, abandonment, danger and fear. Foyer93, like other *foyers-taudis,* will undergo relocation projects in the near future. The residents are not granted any assurances and are likely to face repatriation. Therefore, what are their expectations? What does their life experience at Foyer93 tell us about migrants' well-being and integration in France?

Anthropology of the *Foyers*

Anthropology in France, not unlike in other countries, has from its inception been concerned with the study of either rural and internal or far-distant communities (Bazin et al. 2006). Thus, it has addressed the exotic, the alien and the external, lacking an understanding of the country's internal diversity, which has instead been pushed to the margins. Migration Studies started out by using a structural approach (Noiriel 1988), while more recently social scientists have turned to the migrant communities in France in relation to their involvement in development projects in Africa (Quiminal 2002; Grillo and Bruno 2004). Interestingly, medical-anthropological studies focusing on the health-seeking behaviour of migrants have provided an understanding of the problems they suffer and their social dimensions, but they have also provided a critique of the way that French transcultural psychiatry and French society have engaged with migration. Devereux (1978, 1980) and Nathan (1986) led the way in this regard, filling the gap between psychiatry and medical anthropology (see Chapter 7).

The *foyers*, where people sojourn at times for twenty years or even a lifetime, have been construed as gateways, transit zones or temporary solutions before more permanent accommodation can be achieved, while in reality, they are suspended between the unsatisfactory present and the projection towards better adjustments: new residency permits, a place for a bed, more room in the wardrobe. A sense of blockage seizes those who enter these places, notwithstanding the frenetic activity generally going on at Foyer93. The detachment of the *foyers* from the rest of Paris and even from their own neighbourhoods stigmatises further the people who live there. The *foyers* are as socially invisible as their residents are silent, undergoing the same denial as a part of the French colonial history to which they are a testimony. Meanwhile, the *foyers* have seen the coming and going of different people, and the passing of time has marked these buildings with deterioration.

In a postcolonial fashion, I carried out fieldwork in one of these *foyers* because the anthropologist there acts as a broker, allowing life stories and people to speak for themselves (if this can ever be achieved) to the wider public. Certainly, I had to be legitimised by my respondents to do so; they accepted me and my work under the impulse of their increasing awareness of the misrepresentation and prejudice that the wider public held towards the Muslim community and migrants by and large. Despite my own reservations about their possible response to me carrying out fieldwork in the *foyer* and the general lack of mobilisation within Foyer93, the residents needed to be heard and to talk. This, which is also a finding of medical associations working in the *foyers*, reveals the residents' psychological need to be listened to beyond the group spectacle, which depicts them as a community of people always clustered together. Their 'African-style' community life is nothing more than the lack of privacy induced by the overcrowding of the *foyers*, and is thus a sign of their marginalisation. The residents complain and are very vociferous about this. What are the channels that they use to express themselves in a situation already curtailed by illegality, isolation and poverty? What are the margins of marginality? Is Islam indeed the fundamental issue among the residents of Foyer93, as the political discourse would imply?

The features of present-day migration have changed greatly in recent years. As Wihtol de Wenden (2001) has argued, there are almost as many forms of migration as there are migrants themselves. Any migratory project is unique in itself; strategies overlap at moments in time, without being final, univocal choices. The old 'migratory couples', as Wihtol de Wenden defined them, that is, the movement from the ex-colonies to the ex-colonial powers, for instance between France and West Africa or the United Kingdom and the countries of the Commonwealth, are no longer the main points of either arrival or departure. It appears that the poorest countries in Africa are turning towards nearer countries on the same continent; that sending Mediterranean countries, such as Spain and Italy, have turned into receiving countries; and that the 'pull' factors of migration have taken precedence over the 'push' factors (ibid.), meaning that the attractiveness of the richest countries has become a reason in itself to emigrate, without necessarily being linked to the poverty of one's home country. The typologies of migration may also fall within different categories, ranging from spatial (national and transnational, diasporic) to social and cultural ones, such as gender, age, social status and so on – not to mention readings of the phenomenon in economic, political or demographic terms.

Mobility is no longer limited in time as it was in the past (e.g. seasonal migration in Africa or temporary labour work in the factories of Europe). The 1974 border restrictions in France made people believe that migration would gradually stop, or that only elite migrants would be able to migrate easily. Nonetheless, migration has remained constant. In addition, the image of the migrant is not entirely that of the rural migrant, coming from the village without schooling. Indeed, illegal migrants are also middle-class people who have come to Europe in the hope of advancing their careers. However, while this is the general trend in Europe, my fieldwork data in the *foyer* revealed quite widespread illiteracy and traditional ways of life, especially considering that the majority of my respondents are from the rural region of Kayes, Mali. What is profiled is a new form of conflict (Agier 2011), which sees free circulation and the possibility of finding a new place in the world hindered. The myth of transnational movement enabled by globalisation can only but deceive those who decide to take the plunge, who find themselves stopped by the ever-increasing legal restrictions for non-Schengen countries. Migrants and asylum seekers alike are rejected at the borders, placed in immigration detention centres (Könönen 2021) or ending up in the *foyers*. Are these migrants the real face of globalisation?

As the landscape of migration maps onto marginalisation, poor housing and instability, the *foyers de travailleurs migrants* (housing for migrant workers) resonate with the idea of circulation as being dysfunctional in itself, rather than with quaint forms of living that are seemingly frozen in time. West African migrants bring back the notion of cosmopolitanism through non-elite strategies of survival in the face of insecurity (Kothari 2008), which create temporal niches within the wider global phenomenon of migration. However, free circulation is granted to goods, not to people. This being the case, the capitalist ideal has fully established itself, and with it, its inevitable alienation. People are goods; as such, they are sellable, usable and susceptible to being returned to the sender. Foyer93 stores its residents, like a warehouse stores its merchandise, stacking them in room-dormitories, assigning them both a location and an expiry date: the residents are expected to leave Foyer93 in time, moving on to either private accommodation or back to their homelands.

Hence, diasporic trends have become transnational and return migration less viable because of tighter European legislation towards non-EU citizens, while international networks have strengthened. Migrants can in fact only return to their countries when their legal status is cleared, such that many prefer to remain in the liminal space of illegality rather than risking being refused entry upon their return to France (personal communication). Therefore, they maintain links with their homeland through religious centres, migrants' associations and by phone. The current economic recession and pandemic-induced isolation worldwide can only have reinforced this trend. All the while, the hypothesis according to which religion would disappear or be privatised (Habermas 1991) as a result of modernisation and secularisation processes has not proved to be tenable. AfterHefner (1998: 87), we know that the vibrant resurgence of religious movements in the West during the Enlightenment was supported by a 'newly urbanized working and middle-class', and per Gellner (1992), that nationhood corresponded in Muslim countries to a return to Islam through the purification of religion. In France, from the foundation of the Republic, the secular and religious domains were to remain separate, and religion was to pertain to the private realm of human agency, which no survey could ever breach. Paradoxically, this has not generated more respect for the other's faith, but rather more suspicion, prejudice and confusion, and has led to religion receiving greater visibility in the public domain.

France and Islam: A Contested Relationship

As much as the September 11 attack on the Twin Towers in New York indelibly marked our memories, so has the 13 November 2015 explosion at the Bataclan music venue in Paris, with the power of a disruptive violence that has reawakened[7] a counter-logic of resentment and closure towards Muslim communities in the West. Public discourse worldwide has made national security its prime political objective and transformed Muslim communities into potential suspects. The long-standing relationship between France and Islam, which goes back to colonial times, is caught in a stalemate in which diffidence and fear have increased on both sides. Anthropological work among Muslim communities in France has changed drastically, with African respondents less and less willing to cooperate with anthropologists. African Studies have declined in favour of wider perspectives turned towards Cultural Studies, Religious and Globalisation Studies, while the discourse about migration has gradually moved from an economic approach to one of national security regarding Islam. Recently, the Brexit campaign and Donald Trump's presidential campaigns respectively have tapped into a blunt sense of generalised instability, for which Muslim migrants are blamed, in order to divide the electorate and successfully defeat leftist or inclusive views of society. Thus, migration from the ex-colonies is no longer, or not simply, a matter of cultural difference, expressed harmoniously or through clashes according to Huntington's analysis (1996), but one which emphasises Islam in particular as the Pandora's box of our time. While internationally, Islam is associated with extremism and terrorism, in France it is drawn into an oppositional debate in which Muslims, as bearers of religious sectarianism and *communautarisme*, community drift, would infringe upon the Republican value of *laïcité*, secularism. Islam appears to be the central issue, since it is by drawing on it that Muslims claim their identity in the diaspora and French republicanism articulates its discourse in order to integrate or eschew the influx of Muslim migrants onto French soil (Mayanthi 2014). Migration, Islam and identity were the buzzwords during the time of the riots in the French banlieues[8] (October–November 2005), when angry French youths expressed their rage at the exclusionary French policies that targeted, in their view, people of migrant descent. Islam in France is the prism through which integration, ethnicity and religion take form, albeit in disguise. In fact, assimilation, community and *communautarisme* are used as substitutes for these concepts, or rather as the French versions of them. In turn, the community members of my study, through a discourse connecting the *sans-papiers* (undocumented migrants) to the *tirailleurs* (Senegalese and Malian veterans), uphold/exhibit a postcolonial legacy based on traditional ideas of 'trans-generational mutual obligations' (Mann 2003: 377).

The moment of social crisis during which my fieldwork took place – although potentially a threat to my entire work – also presented an ideal perspective that enabled me to observe the conflict in action, the positions emerge and the debate develop. The 2005 uprisings in the suburbs of France and the Île-de-France region violently brought the migrant community, both old and new, back into the spotlight, and in unmitigatedly negative terms. Suburban Paris was equated with disaffected people, generally migrants or French people of migrant descent, and with Muslims. Islam became a synonym for Salafism, used to indicate radical Islam that was attempting to reform Islam first and then the West by referring to literal understandings of the Qur'an and by enforcing strict forms of behaviour and dressing. However, the discontent was not voiced in the jargon of Islam, nor did Muslim leaders – Algerian qadis or West African marabouts – take the forefront. The crisis did not have the characteristics of a movement, but featured only groups of disenfranchised youths, who vandalised cars and verbally assaulted transport workers for symbolising the system that denied them any kind of social 'mobility'. Their violence originated elsewhere.

The uprisings flagged the discontent of the French working class, many of whom are indeed Muslim and of migrant descent, and who were symbolically aligned with the new migrants, also supposedly Muslims. Thus, a reconsideration of the role of Islam in France was inevitable, going beyond the security issues that the crisis had highlighted. At the same time, positive action was implemented in the suburbs to help the youths from disadvantaged boroughs find jobs in Paris, where they were notoriously turned down. The face of France and the identity of its citizens had to be reconsidered at a national level. The *foyers*, such as Foyer93, which could have become hotbeds of resistance and contestation, remained silent and quiescent. No mention of them was made in the national press, while they continue to exist in their state of segregation. Nonetheless, discussions did take place among the residents, reflecting their anxieties and hopes about their future, since the migrant community in France is defined primarily as Muslim, thus contradicting the notion that secularism regards people as equal individuals, shorn of ethnic, gender and religious connotations.

Islam is now the second religion of France, after Catholicism and above Judaism and Buddhism, with about five and a half million Muslims living in the country.[9] Since the period of its colonies in Africa (West Africa, Algeria and the Moroccan protectorate), France has been confronted with Islam. With the formation of French West Africa (Afrique Occidentale Française), comprising what are now the states of Senegal and Mali, France aimed at dealing peacefully with the local Muslim realities in order to obtain the people's support and cooperation. Coppolani and Depont (1897) initiated anthropological studies on what they defined as *Black* Islam, central to the understanding and control of the Muslim countries. Coppolani, posted in Algeria, worked for the colonial administration with 'a very strong military orientation' (Robinson 2000b: 32). His writings were the main reference for the understanding of Islam in Africa until postcolonial studies attacked them for being imprecise and ethnocentric.

The search for the 'other' in anthropology has reached a point of exhaustion due to the homogenising phenomenon of globalisation, which has rendered the world uniform in 'aspirations and mode of thought' (Littlewood 2003: 256). The 'other' can no longer be found in the idealised romantic image of distant tribes whose practices are unknown and alien to ours, if not in meaning and intentions. Nonetheless, the Muslim 'phenomenon' appears to have taken on those characteristics, so as to become something totally non-Western, anti-progressive and radically different. The challenge that lies ahead concerns how French universalism will be able to fine-tune itself in order to accommodate the varieties of communities and the plethora of Islamic tendencies in and of France. In this book I will show, by analysing the Sufi Mouride community of the Île-de-France region, how the country is headed towards a successful acknowledgement of its Muslim citizens and their expressions of faith.

Outline of the Book

This book is an anthropological contribution to the field of migration studies in that it builds on issues of well-being and community-making among sub-Saharan minority groups in France. It takes its cue from the social life and health-seeking behaviour of the *foyer* residents, to whom my interest was drawn to analyse issues of integration as part of the French national controversy on migration and Islam. The Mouride[10] brotherhood, founded in Senegal by Cheick Amadou Bamba M'Backé (1855–1927), serves to broaden the view of Islam in Paris as one of its many faces, and to show how Muslim allegiances are changing in relation to the homeland. Debates surrounding migration are often equated with Islam and seem to have veered towards the Muslims' home countries, their own development and their peace-making, while France attempts to reaffirm its presence on the international scene by promoting the value of *francophonie*, conceived of as a cultural world, sharing a common heritage, with French as a common language. This is all the more salient with regard to Africa, as the Francophone world lies now, more than ever, on the circulation of both its values and interlocutors in and from Francophone Africa, an economically, demographically and culturally growing area. Sub-Saharan migrations are in fact characterised by the geopolitical dimension of *francophonie*, as partially are those from the Maghreb as well, where French is generally the second national language after Arabic.

    In Chapter 1, I examine the historical backdrop to current migration issues in reference to the integration of the 'second generation' (people born to migrant parents). This sociological category was first used with reference to the Algerians and the problem that their children posed as new Muslims citizens of France. This was in the years following the 1974 law, which closed the doors to migration and family reunions and was the first example of what is now the European utopia of zero migration, implemented by the Schengen treaty. I provide an overview of France's relationship with its colonies in order to understand the way in which it grappled with Islam and the Muslims there, before this became a domestic French issue. The Soninkés are an old migratory group to France (they are now into their third generation) that has nevertheless remained in the shadows. In Chapter 2, I show how I resolved to work at Foyer93. In Chapter 3, I introduce the *foyer*-space as it was originally conceived and as it presents itself now, in order to ground and give context to the residents' narratives and everyday lives, which I shared, with the caveats and limitations of carrying out fieldwork as a woman among uniquely single male migrants. The constraints of the *foyer* create a hybrid tradition, combining village roles with necessity and improvisation. The old residents and their migratory practices, now gradually being abandoned, testify to the role they played in shaping current migration. The analysis of Foyer93 continues in Chapter 4, where I assess the Soninkés' practice of Islam, which is composite and plural. Next to the clerical figure of the leader of prayer, the imam, stand the spiritual leader or marabout and the iron-makers, who both perform divination and have a relationship with the jinns, the spirits. Both claim to practise in the cadre of Islam, either because they have a relationship with Muslim spirits or because they employ ritual formulas drawn from the Qur'an (or both). While within the Mouride community (the object of Chapter 5 and 6) a strong Sufi theodicy assigns everyone their role (spiritual and mundane), the same cannot be said for the Soninké community at Foyer93. The Mouride order has a long history dating back to the foundation of the *tariqa* (الطريقة), or Sufi order – which continues and thrives in the diaspora too. The Mouride community has been able to settle in France and to be an important feature of the consolidating *French* Islam, quite in resonance with the French goal of bringing Islam into the folds of the Republic. In Chapter 7, the French understanding and provision of health is outlined and countered by a case study of ritual healing. Finally, I draw my conclusions on the status quo of both French minority groups and Islam in France, together with their achievements and setbacks.

Notes

1. This ethnic group lives in the regions between Senegal and Mali along the Senegal River Valley, and is a subdominant group (demographically and linguistically) in both states: the Wolof ethnic group is dominant in Senegal, while the Bambara are dominant in Mali. The Soninké are part of the wider Mande family group, comprising the Bambara and the Mandinka.
2. A *foyer* refers to housing exclusively for single male migrants.

3. The Beurs movement of the 1970s involved the uprising of the Parisian banlieues through the organised action of French youths of Algerian origin, claiming civil rights and political recognition. It also involved a great number of Algerian migrants living in SONACOTRA *foyers*. The movement is tragically remembered for the fierce oppression of the protesters at the hands of the French gendarmes.

4. The *foyers* benefit from the L633-1 Article of Construction and Housing (2000 Law), according to which they are private domiciles, whose internal organisation cannot be subjected to restrictions 'other than those fixed by the law'. Thus, the residents enjoy considerable freedom at (and control over) the *foyers*.

5. Sub-Saharan migration to OECD countries, estimated to 3.4 million migrants (with only 300 thousand in France), is inferior to the overall stock that reached 7.2 million Africans in 2000, https://www.oecd.org/els/mig/Beauchemin.pdf.

6. South-South migrations are equivalent to 36% of the total stock of migrants, amounting to 90.2 million, https://www.oecd.org/dev/migration-development/south-south-migration.htm

7. The Al-Qaida Islamic terrorist network attacked in the United States first (11 September 2001) and Europe later, with sequels in Madrid (11 March 2004) and London (7 July 2005). ISIS has since claimed victims in Berlin (19 December 2016), London (several attacks in 2017) and throughout France (since 2014), with the last episode on 24 May 2019 in Lyon that has been treated as a case of terrorism.

8. The banlieue, which literally means *lieu bannis*, or 'banned place', is first of all a peripheral territory, where different socio-economic realities coexist. The banlieues have a wider meaning than 'outskirts of a town' or 'suburbs'. They comprise the departments surrounding the capital city of a region and include smaller communes. Nonetheless, I will use the words 'suburb' and 'banlieue' as synonyms.

9. See https://fr.statista.com/statistiques/472017/population-religion-france/ (accessed 28 Mars 2022).

10. *Mouridullah* (مريد الله) refers to the Sufi faithful, following the path to God.

1

A Blast from the Past

West African Migration to France

Migration, although always considered an external phenomenon to France (Rosenberg 2006), has been structural since the Franco-Prussian War, when the recruitment of new citizens and thus of soldiers able to fight for the French side became vital.[1] In 1889, France started to perceive itself as a country of immigration rather than emigration, such that the nation gave way to the state, while the principle of *jus soli* was introduced and added to that of *jus sanguinis*; England enforced it shortly before France, while Germany did so only in 2000 (Weil 2008). Following the aftermath of the Second World War and up until the 1960s, labour migration was significant in European countries, such as Spain, where Muslim migrants have also become an important presence, as well as Portuguese and Italian migrants have in France.[2] In 2004, migration from sub-Saharan countries represented only 12 per cent of the overall migrant input to France – notwithstanding its growth from two thousand migrants in 1962 to 570,000 in 2004 (Lessault and Beauchemin 2009) – yet its history, and that of the Soninkés' migration from the Senegal River Valley, spanning the countries of Mali, Mauritania and Senegal, is long (Gnisci and Trémolières 2006). Senegalese migration, predominantly of the Wolof ethnic group, is more recent (see Chapters 5 and 6). It dates from the late 1960s and was particularly spurred on by the droughts of the early 1970s that affected most of the Sahelian regions. Strictly speaking, these were the first climate refugee movements in history, not considering the Italian mass migration to the Americas at the end of the nineteenth century.[3]

Mobility in Africa is a key feature and an economic strategy, 'historically embedded in Sahelian cultures, marked by a high degree of opportunistic' choices (De Bruijn et al. 2001: 65). Three phases can be outlined: the first encompassed the enrolment of African people, including the Soninkés *navetans*, sailors recruited by maritime companies serving the West African coasts (Manchuelle 1997). This was possible throughout the period between the First and Second World Wars, when the introduction of diesel made the unpleasant work of African coal-trimmers and stokers unnecessary, and preference was instead given to French nationals. 'By the 1970s all the Soninké sailors had become *postals*, waiters' (ibid.:201). It was in the 1960s, with a flourishing economy and an insufficient labour force (due to the Algerian War), that France seemed to 'discover' its African migrants. A multilateral pact was signed in 1962 allowing migrants from West Africa free circulation and imposing no restrictions on their stay in France or their employment. Economic agents recruited labour in situ, in the entire region of the Senegal River Valley (Diop 1993: 118). This was the second phase of West African migration, called *noria*, or circular migration. Migrants worked for periods of four or five years and then returned home, and were replaced by their next of kin. The third phase comprised the movement of Senegalese students and peddlers (both predominantly affiliated to the Mouride brotherhood, and to a lesser degree also to the Tijaniyya), together with the new component of refugees from countries such as the Congo, Zaire, Angola and Guinea-Bissau (ibid.).

While development in Africa presupposes an ever-increasing presence of French business in the region of Kayes, which is rich in natural resources (diamonds and gold), migration from the 'Muslim countries' has made Islam the focal point through which new political configurations and discourses shape multiculturalism, in France as throughout the West.

Multiculturalism and Islam

Over at least the past two decades, multiculturalism has become part of the European political agenda concerning the definition of its political and cultural identity, in which Islam can be the grounds for denial of EU membership for security reasons. Such was the case of Turkey. While the constitution of the European community opened up a process of inclusion and expansion, each country has created its own internal distinctions as to what citizenship should be and to whom it should be granted. The distinction between what is external and internal has blurred in the face of Muslim communities claiming citizenship and equal rights. Certainly, the first step towards the inclusion and recognition of Muslim communities has been the institutionalisation of the Muslim faith, which occurred in France in 1926 with the foundation of the French Council of the Muslim Faith; nonetheless, the matter is not solely legal, but deeply steeped in the social and cultural habits that these institutions represent. This is why the Muslim community in Europe has claimed the principle, through the Association of Imams of France, of a sharia for minority groups, advocating the self-regulation of Muslim minority groups in the nation states where they live as citizens or migrants (Frégosi 2005: 108). Not dissimilar is the European Council of Fatwas and Research, founded in 1997 in Great Britain, equipped with two regional commissions in the UK and France (ibid.: 107).

Muslim minority groups have become economic actors, for example in Germany, where self-employed Turks have created their own small-scale businesses (Pécoud 2004), so that a kind of multiculturalism rooted in economic viability has come forward. Yet again, the openness of global markets, and the mobility of people, conflict with the internal regulations of each country, serving to reinforce the sovereignty of the nation states rather than dissolving it, as the former would imply. In addition, migration and the settling of migrants in Europe (and worldwide) does not only bring successful entrepreneurs or intellectuals – the Sarkosian idea of *migration choisie*, or selected migration, related to the phenomenon of brain drain – but also people in search of a better life, such that elite migrants are but a small minority.

Muslim minority groups have been the object of racism and discrimination, often because they correspond to the outcast proletariat of great cities, where they are lumped together and where education, access to services and decent housing are impaired. In France, a policy of positive action has been implemented since the 1980s in the Zones of Priority Education (ZEPs), the banlieues, where pedagogic and social insertion programmes have aimed at the 'integration' of these groups, which are understood as 'minorités ethniques à problème', problematic minorities (Wihtol de Wenden 2005). The acknowledgement of the existence of ethnic groups in France has come through the recognition of their social malaise, and thus through their stigmatisation (Littlewood and Lipsedge 2004). The historical background to this is the 1960s, when the housing crisis and the baby boom brought about the construction of large, built-up areas for low-rent housing – the Habitation à Loyer Moderé (HLM) – after Le Corbusier's popular model, where young couples settled and started their new lives. Migrants from West Africa and Algerians of the second generation robustly ethnicised these territories, making them less appealing to the French middle and lower classes – the *français de souche*, as they are normally referred to, who gradually deserted these areas. The banlieues then began to attract only migrants from the bidonvilles and the run-down areas of the metropolis (Tetreault 2015). The configuration Île-de-France region is thus a world in which the unblemished rigor of class and ethnicity works to make these areas into the lost territories of the Republic, as Brenner (2002) famously sketched them.

The emergence of communities *issues de la migration* (born out of migration) has brought about the rethinking of the French national identity. Muslim minority groups, guilty of introducing their *communautarisme* through their customs and Islam itself – the one a synonym of the other – defy the Republican model, which is liberal, democratic and secular in nature. These fundamentals were the crux of the political debate about access to citizenship and the reform of the National Code from 1987 to 1993. The year 1989 saw the foulard affair, followed by the foundation of the Haute Conseil à l'Integration in 1991, created to decide the criteria by which identity (religious and civic) corresponded to the French model (Kastoryano 2006: 58). Arguably, community-based representations were obliterated, and with them, multiculturalism.

The construction of the Great Mosque of Paris was also an attempt to institutionalise and give unity to the plethora of Muslim actors in France, as well 'as a gesture of gratitude for the Muslim soldiers who died fighting for France in World War I' (ibid.:101). Since the traumatic events of Independence in the ex-colonies, not only did France have to redesign its overseas territories (France d'Outre-Mer), but succeeding governments have had to recontextualise Islam and the Muslim population in France: migration from the ex-colonies had transformed them into a domestic issue, such that a redefinition of the concept of citizenship was underway through this modern conflict staging, as it were, enlightened secularists and obscurantist Muslims, who now shared the same nationality.

It is worth mentioning that traditionally, multiculturalism was never advocated in France, where, since the Napoleonic Code, the concern has always been towards achieving national unity. The school (as much as the army) has had a prime role in the formation of a unified cultural system. The uniformity of shared cultural values to which citizens conform is also what constitutes the basis for an assimilative model of integration, such as the one that France has practised so far. Thus, Muslims should abandon their customs and embrace a French way of life (that is, they should speak French, attend French schools, abandon the hijab in public spaces and so forth). Only through this process of adaptation do Muslim communities have a chance to become, and to be seen as becoming, French citizens. How this plays out on the ground for my sample community is what I intend to show in the following chapters.

Integration, Super-diversity and Heterotopias

As Modood (2006) has pointed out, the Muslim community in Britain has been central in the critique of liberal ideas of racial equality, towards a more nuanced multiculturalism based on the right to one's difference, including religious difference. In Britain, in fact, colour and 'race' constituted the only grounds for illegal discrimination and racism until 2003, when an offence of religious discrimination was introduced (ibid.: 38). Modood casts Muslim assertiveness in the wider political ferment of identity movements, such as feminism and LGBT activism, which go against universalistic conceptions of justice and the individual. Similarly, Foucault and Derrida's anti-essentialism was used in France to criticise hegemonic formulations of gender, class and so forth (ibid.: 40), so that the integration of Muslim communities in France fits in with feminist ideas of difference and separate development (Strathern 1987, 2004, 2016).

The first theory of integration, positing adaptation or conformism to the shared good, can be identified with the Chicago School of sociology, with exemplars such as Park and Burgess (1921) and Bateson (1935), while the second is that of segmented assimilation – or differential integration, as Zehraoui (1996) put it – as conceptualised by Portes (Portes and Borocz 1989; Portes and Sensenbrenner 1993; Portes and Zhou 1993). Portes's triadic model put forward the following situations: the first is the classic, Republican idea of integration, maintaining that the individual should conform to both the economic and cultural values of the host community, which serve as signs of their successful integration and thus of their upward mobility. Sayad (1979, 1999) underlined the ethnocentric and colonial heritage of such an approach, which frames the migrant's ethnic background as something that hinders their full integration. Tribalat (1996), who has provided the only quantitative data existing in France on the subject, takes the case of West Africans and Algerians, who present a strong element of cultural mixing (through marriage, housing and other aspects), but also have little social capital. This situation is exemplified by Portes's (1995) second model of integration, called downward integration. The Portuguese community in

France, characterised by economic viability, but also strong community bonds and little mixing (Safi 2006: 8), corresponds to the third model. This theory may answer to both multiculturalist (against the idea of a unified cultural system) and structuralist (according to which society exhibits different social classes and inequalities) understandings of integration, especially when different groups are involved.

However, current international circulations have questioned methodological nationalism (i.e. inclusion/marginalisation issues addressed as a specific national context) through a focus on transnational and diasporic issues (Ali-Bencherif et al. 2019; Fábos 2008; Trovão 2014; Schönwälder et al. 2016), while transit migrations have redefined the logics of departure, destination and return, and transformed today's migrants into a hybrid category. Sociocultural and ecological patterns are rapidly changing, while research in all disciplines is faced with the quandary of paradigm shifts that defy earlier sociological approaches to the phenomenon (Miller et al. 2008). In the field of Migration Studies, the concept of super-diversity has been employed to think of current migration as 'a kind of complexity surpassing anything previously experienced in a particular society' (Vertovec 2007, 2019); this is a concept that could grasp the multitude of issues that migration brings into analysis, and that has ultimately moved the debate from questions of integration to those of interaction, while relationships have become increasingly more cosmopolitan and complex. Arguably, the paradox of our current global era is that of having created, if nothing else, transcultural places (Rhazzali 2015), understood as social and political markers that are constantly redefined by different cultural reconfigurations (Accoroni 2018). *Mutatis mutandis*, 'the characteristic of integration, which everybody is after, is that it can only be achieved as a secondary effect of actions undertaken for other purposes' (Sayad 1994: 13).

Thus, in what sense are the residents of Foyer93 important to current anthropological work on migration and Islam? Do they reintroduce the problem of the *sans-papiers* into the public debate, or that of the racism to which the descendants of migrants are subjected? Migrants, although much discussed in the media, remain an invisible and silent group of people, whose marginalisation is not accidental, but rather socially constructed subordination (Gilroy 1992). Especially after 9/11, the loyalty of Muslim diasporic groups (settled minority groups and migrants) has been questioned (Werbner 2004), so much so that living in the diaspora is ultimately a constant negotiation of 'the parameters of minority citizenship' (ibid.: 471). As early as 1967, Foucault talked of heterotopias (ibid.: 1986)[4], that is, of all other spaces that in contrast to utopias, with no real place in the world, mirror ordinary places by subverting and overturning them. Heterotopias are for example cemeteries, reminding the living of death, of time's rupture and decomposition. From the nineteenth century onwards, in order to avoid contamination and sickness, they were moved from a central position within the town to its outskirts. One other classification that may be useful to our understanding of the *foyers* is Foucault's fifth example of heterotopias: the close and isolated spaces that one cannot penetrate unless one is forced to (e.g. a prison) or where a rite of purification is implied (the Muslim hammam; we could also add the mosque to this category). Brothels, colonies, hospitals and so forth are also heterotopias, spaces regulated by meaning, such as the perfect Jesuit settlements in South America, whose spatial organisation had marked 'the geography of the American world' with Christianity (ibid.: 26). As I see it, the *foyers*, as much as the banlieues, may be another type of Foucauldian heterotopia, at times encompassing them all. They are closed spaces where the migrant is forced to remain, but they are also places of rescue for both those who inhabit them and for the wider community, which can thus keep them at bay. Their proximity and visibility are dangerous, and they are a reminder of another heterotopia: the colony, which should be far away.

Migration has subverted the logic of distance, even beyond globalisation, which has granted worldwide networking and free movement to things, but not to people. It has brought a piece of colonial memory before Republican eyes. The impossibility of defining the *foyers* with the mark of the Republic generates disapproval, rejection, denial and disgust. Even at the heart of Paris, the *foyers* remain invisible entities, cast out of the main social body and thus regaining the distance that they are expected to entail as absolute others. Not only is an aesthetics of conformity underway, but also a moral one, after which recognising the *foyers* would equate to becoming conscious that a negotiation is due; that probably, 'these others' within the Republic demonstrate that the universal principle of unity is at issue and needs revising. At present, however, the *foyers* are merely heterotopias of unwanted migration.

Not So 'Off the Veranda'

At the start of my fieldwork, my focus was on Sufi healing practices among the Senegalese community in Paris. To this end, I undertook a pilot period of fieldwork of a few months to obtain contacts and access among the Mouride community members. During the first months, I therefore based my investigation at the Mouride Islamic Centre of Taverny in the Île-de-France region, and was unaware of the existence of the *foyers*. My country of origin, Italy, has something similar in Brescia, where one housing centre accommodates Senegalese families. Yet the uniqueness of Foyer93 is in both its quaintness and its complete absence of women and children.

I soon realised that at the Mouride Islamic Centre, I would acquire knowledge about Islam and about the theodicy of this Sufi branch, but certainly not an entry into the community itself and its members' homes, and even less into the lives of the most vulnerable migrants, who attend the centre very sporadically or whose anonymity the centre has to protect. This approach nevertheless guaranteed me the possibility of analysing one of the many facets of Islam in France, and the adjustments and new reconfigurations it has undergone.

Clearly, urban anthropology does not correspond to the romantic Malinowskian ideal prompting the researcher to get off his veranda and fling himself off to far-distant countries to be soon incorporated into the life of the community under study[5]. The 'cargo cult' is prehistory in anthropology, as is the idea it conveys of primordial encounters with peoples inhabiting completely separate worlds (Gupta and Ferguson 1997). Senegal and Mali have been subject to French colonial power since the time of Afrique Occidentale Française (AOF), which had Bamako as its capital. During this time, Sufi West African leaders – the marabouts – were subjugated, deported or eventually cooperated with the French administration. Senegalese and Malian minority groups in France resent the part that France has played in the making of their history up to now. The 2005 riots have become paradigmatic of this, hence these groups' privacy and overall suspicion of the wider (white) community. The same goes for researchers, who are regarded broadly as journalists of a kind, spying into their lives only to depict them negatively, summarily or wrongly. Episodes of previous research carried out in the *foyers*, for example, have led to police raids and awakened a sensationalist interest from the media, which of course the community concerned did not appreciate. As my respondents reminded me later on, working in Senegal or Mali might have proved relatively easy for me, because my research participants would have been in their home country, where researchers are met with greater favour than in France, where the relationship is reversed and, most of all, where migrants endure marginalisation and discrimination. In sum, my idea of getting access to the Mouride community via their religious centre revealed itself to be a dream at best.

It became clear that I had to be part of a social network that included both French people and West African migrants; a middle ground that enabled both groups to come together transparently. In that way, I would gain a form of recognition and the community's trust, which would eventually constitute my only way in. I therefore resorted to grassroots associations working on migration and health, which remained part of my research focus. I gathered information on the main organisations working with migrants in this field and on those ones run by migrants themselves. I eventually chose four among these, which not only made my research in Paris possible, but gave it another direction. More than providing invaluable insights into my work on the ground, these organisations became part of my research. The social workers and volunteers working for them exhibited a dissenting humanscape, pivoted around the *foyers* in support, solidarity and ultimately critique of an otherwise unchecked discriminatory system affecting the migrants.

Transnationalism, Economic Development and Migrants' Associations

Migration, transnationalism and economic development are deeply interrelated, so that a number of works in the social sciences have been dedicated to the effervescence of migrants' associations, which in France was the result of the 1981 law that lifted the ban of the 1939 law preventing migrants from creating associations; this enabled the emergence of a plethora of migrant associations, including religious ones. Their novelty lies in the centrality of the migrants' involvement, beyond the bilateral programmes of the states or NGOs concerned.

For the first time, this phenomenon attracted the attention of French anthropologists, such as Quiminal (1991), who put forward the concept of translocality, summed up by the image of 'ici et là-bas' ('here and there'), also reflected in the title of her seminal work. The aforementioned statistical marginality of West African migration to France does not account for the fact that virtually every Soninké family in the Senegal River Valley has at least one member who is a migrant, and that West African migrants have responded to global economic and political challenges (e.g. the tightening of migration laws worldwide) by becoming primary agents for the progress of their home countries through economic cooperation (Sarr 2009).

At Foyer93, the initiatives related to development in Mali appeal to the residents, who get involved in cooperation projects with existing French associations. The Groupe de Recherches et de Réalisations pour le Développement Rural (GRDR) has established a strong link with Sadiola, Kayes, for example, where the most important gold mine of the region is. Similarly, the Association pour la Formation Technique des Africaines et Malgaches (AFTAM) has become a partner in a project called

Telemigrants, launched in 2006 by the group Telemedia as the outcome of meetings held in Lyon for the 'digital linking' of migrants with their home countries. This project was carried out through the intervention of the Ministry of Immigration, Integration and National Identity and of Social Development to benefit the urban centres of Kersiniané and Yelimané in Mali. The group funded up to 57 per cent of the cost relative to the study and implementation of the project, which would have been too demanding for its beneficiaries to cover. With the cooperation of the Worldwide Francophone Digital University (UFDM) and the Worldwide Agency for Digital Solidarity (ASDM), two subprojects have been launched: distance learning and health prevention programmes. At the time of my fieldwork, the opening of an internet and long-distance call centre adjacent to Foyer93 was also in the works. Nonetheless, with the incumbent dismantling of Foyer93, all these projects have evaporated.

Traoré, 42, a resident of Foyer93, one of the Sages[6] and also *chef du village* at Yelimané, is one of the beneficiaries of the Telemigrants project. Two other people at Foyer93, also from Yelimané, participated in the project with him, while networking with other people in the village. So far, only projects of this kind have been pursued: with the funding available, the migrants and the local mayors (in Paris and Kayes) find better outcomes and in a shorter time than are achieved through health projects. The creation of an internet point at Yelimané, for example, provided a source of revenue for those working at it, as well as the members of their families and those belonging to the migrants' associations in Mali, beyond the obvious expediency of a centre of this kind. On the day preceding his departure to Mali for the inauguration of the project, Traoré indulged in the court next to the market stand, where it is easy to stop for a quick chat, with the excuse of buying kola nuts or sticks used for tooth-cleaning. He wore a brown cowboy hat, a visible sign of success, tangibly signalling a change in his life. I greeted him and he told me about his departure to Yelimané: the time had come for him to mark his achievement. He was the recipient of the funds provided for the implementation of the project, from which the village would benefit thanks to him.

The *foyer* is not only a place where solidarity can be found; it is also where networking and skills are put into practice. It envisions basic help at the initial stage of one's migratory trajectory, after which each person has equal chances. In a way, Foyer93 marks the passage from Mali to France, as well as from youth to manhood. The success of the migratory project is not the exit from the *foyers* in itself, but the migrant's status within the community, which increasingly means the community in Paris. Traoré, not so young anymore and a traditional leader of his own village, already had status in the eyes of the community. Nonetheless, the residents at Foyer93 are from different villages, and therefore his position as a leader was acknowledged when he moved from being a member of the Sages to a delegate at the Residents Council. The distribution of roles upon migration depends on the migrants' skills and their ability to make themselves indispensable (Quiminal 1990).

The reputation that one may gain at Foyer93 is not necessarily discontinuous from that gained in the village; nonetheless, status there encompasses a wider meaning than simply being able to do something. The community sanctions one's expertise when it entails knowledge and power from which the community can profit. There is a hierarchy of values and a time required to achieve them. This is compounded by an understanding of the endurance necessary to undergo the process, which also tests the value of the person. What migration does, indeed, is to subvert the time frame of one's acquisition of knowledge and its attribution, although not the ordeal involved. How many times have I heard respondents say, with regard to someone's success: 'Gosh, he has suffered! He's gone through hell to get where he is', as if it would otherwise be impossible to condone one's achievement.

There is no time in France. People must quickly and effectively find solutions, even in realms such as the spiritual one, which would traditionally require a life-long apprenticeship. At Foyer93, I have met imams, marabouts and businessmen in their thirties: this would be absolutely inconceivable in Mali. At Foyer93, a Western logic of competition is enacted, which goes against the grain of caste rigidities and divisions. The village community expands and overlaps with the diasporic community in Paris. In the same way that back in the village, it was impossible to go beyond the limits of the community in pursuing one's life project, so it is in France, only the boundaries are now also defined by the constraints and hierarchies of Foyer93, by the Parisian municipality and by French national policies on migration.

State and private funding are mobilised towards profitable co-development projects via the migrants' link with their homeland, thus developing an attractive 'ethnic market'. Nevertheless, migrants mainly achieve financial viability in Paris by setting up their own informal businesses or by working for other people in the community (in little restaurants and shops selling various items – books, spices, fabric and so forth). Makalou, a resident at Foyer93 in his forties, told me that one could always draw on one's own entourage as a resource of either recruits or work. Both residents and ex-residents know that financial success can be temporary and circumstances can turn against them: precarious jobs may suddenly end, projects may fail. The *foyer* can be a place of social advancement, but most importantly, of support. This is why even when the residents have moved out of it and settled in Paris, they will always go back to pay visits. The *foyer* is where their security and intergenerational relations lie.

Notes

1. The Alsace and Lorraine regions were still German from 1871 to 1918, after which they were annexed to France.
2. The Portuguese community is the largest in France, but this subject has not attracted much attention from social scientists.
3. Between 1880 and 1915 about 13 million Italians emigrated to the Americas after the country's reunification, which caused heavy taxation, political turmoil and rural mismanagement, resulting in land exhaustion and poverty.
4. 'Heterotopias' was the basis of a lecture given by Foucault in 1967, later published by the French journal Architecture /Mouvement/ Continuité in 1984 with the title 'Des Espaces Autres'. Here I refer to the English translation that was published in 1986.
5. *Off the Veranda* is a documentary series broadcast in 1986 that traced the stories of the first anthropologists to travel around the world, and in particular of Bronisław Kasper Malinowski (1884–1942), who brought about the end of so-called 'armchair anthropology'. While doing research in New Guinea, he moved from the 'veranda method' of his predecessors to what came to be known after him as the 'participant anthropological method', or fieldwork, now the basis of any anthropological research.
6. The *Comité des Sages* (lit. Committee of Wisemen) is a traditional institution constituted by authoritative elderly people who are called upon to decide over contentious issues among and/or of importance for the community members.

2

In the Field

Migrations et Santé

One of the principal associations working on migrants' health (prevention, assistance, follow-ups and so on) in Paris is Migrations & Santé (henceforth M&S). M&S was created in 1974 in order to document and collect comprehensive material on migrants' health in Paris. To this effect, a Documentation Centre gathers all the data collected on the ground by associations, social workers and medical staff – data on which the journal *Migrations Santé* is based. According to its manifesto, the association aims at 'grasping the anthropological features of the migrant's illness', at understanding, that is, the sociocultural aspects that might influence both the aetiology and resolution of such illnesses. Among other activities, M&S delivers its services to the people living in the *foyers* of the region, the so-called Algerian and Malian *foyers*, and addresses situations of distress and mental illness. Loneliness and depression are reported as the most common pathologies suffered by the residents, but more serious episodes of mental illness may occur. For this reason, over the last few years, M&S has carried out counselling sessions in the *foyers*, liaising with doctors and social workers.

M&S holds meetings with the patients and their families – if they so wish – and avails itself of interpreters when required, as its recipients may speak Arabic and Bambara. M&S also helps the patients by referring them to social services and hospitals and by assisting with, if not carrying out, their administrative paperwork. M&S's grassroots intervention in the *foyers* concerns the prevention of HIV and lung and infectious diseases. Thus, professionals offer information and vaccinations (against diphtheria, tetanus, polio, hepatitis B and the seasonal flu) and pulmonary and general check-ups. Recent arrivals are directed to the Centre Bilan (Centre for General Health Check-Ups) as required on the basis of their check-up results. Another important activity concerns the elderly residents of the *foyers*: their health is looked after and their expectations for their future – be that in France or in their homeland – are listened to; they are also assisted in their administrative procedures to obtain pension benefits.

It is thanks to M&S that I was introduced to Foyer93. I had a meeting with the head of M&S at the central office in Paris, and on that occasion, I was allowed to visit their documentation centre, accurately catalogued and mostly furnished with the anthropological literature on migration and health, together with files and papers on migration laws. It had been suggested that I start out by visiting a few *foyers* to get an idea of what they were like and to decide if they could eventually provide the venue for my future fieldwork. The head of M&S firmly believed that a study of migration in Paris on the subject of integration and well-being should start from there.

I therefore took part in several visits to the *foyers*, both in Paris and in the nearby banlieue, during the so-called *permanences*, that is, M&S's visits to the *foyers*. As I will describe in Chapter 3, the *foyers* are run by associations that depend on state funding. The principal ones are the Societé National de Construction pour les Travailleurs Algerians, (SONACOTRA, funded by the Ministry of the Interior, 1955-1970), the Association pour la Formation Technique de base des Africaines et Malgaches (AFTAM, founded in 1962) and the Soutien Union Dignité Accueil du Travailleur Africain (SOUNDIATA, founded in 1963). The latter two are rather more independent from the state than the first, and promote the migrants' participation in the running of the *foyer*. Through one of the AFTAM activists, I started taking part in residents' meetings in one of the *foyers* in Paris, where everyday management issues were discussed. The residents, the AFTAM representatives and a lawyer, advising the committee on legal matters, were routinely present. After a few meetings, the AFTAM representative, a lady in her fifties, invited me to take part in the opening of a new *foyer*. She explained to me that this new *foyer* would be much smaller than usual. The *foyers* are now at the centre of political controversies as to whether they should be demolished and the people rehoused in smaller units, so as to get rid of the most antiquated ones and take stronger control over the residents (migrants).

The residents and several social workers from the region took part in the opening. A few French locals also showed up, which was a rare event, since non-African people rarely visit the *foyers* unless they are social workers or other professionals. Anthropologists, especially women like me, are even fewer and further between. While dilly-dallying, consuming the festive meal that had been served and enjoying the play improvised by one of the residents for the children – from the community and those of the neighbourhood – I met one of the volunteers working at Foyer93 as a teacher of French. She humoured us, saying that a good set of survival skills is necessary to work there, as she lamented the residents' scarce attendance at her lessons and the discomfort of the teaching room, swarmed by cockroaches.

On our way back to Paris, I asked the AFTAM activist if she could show me Foyer93. We made a detour, since it is clustered in a small side street. It is a huge, tall building, overlooking the smaller ones around it. The place is gritty and sombre, sticking out gloomily and grotesquely against the surrounding environment. Certainly, it is not a place where one feels comfortable. To work in such an environment, one required, as the volunteer had ironically stated earlier that afternoon, strong commitment, dedication and empathy for the people who live there on a daily basis. I understood then that the volunteer had neither exaggerated nor made fun of the residents, but simply used a coping trope that whoever attended Foyer93 regularly embraced, including myself in the months to come. Foyer93 had an immediate impact on me. I therefore asked permission to carry out fieldwork there as one of M&S's members. This would give me status vis-à-vis the representative of the residents at Foyer93, the *délégué* (a Soninké resident himself), who, in turn, would authorise my access to the *foyer*. M&S's head offered her and M&S's complete and ongoing support. In the end, a few months from the start of my fieldwork, I finally attended Foyer93 with M&S's and the *délégué*'s endorsement.

My first visit was shocking in many respects, but reinforced all the same my intention to carry on. The physical space looked like a representation of a Malian household (see the following chapter) that happened to have been flung from Kayes into France. The court in the middle of the surrounding living areas – going up three stories from two different entrances, one near the prayer room, the other next to the canteen – made me feel as if I was not just entering a building, but rather the house of quite a large family, huddling all of its members together. My impression was later confirmed by my respondents, who lamented the lack of privacy, but also praised the sense of belonging and cohesion that such an environment provided. The market stands around the perimeter of the court, selling all sorts of religious and lay paraphernalia;

the forge, producing jewellery, the tailor's workshop, the bar and so on depicted at a glance the life that the residents led in Paris.

Their material culture was already in front of me. I later found out that Foyer93 has continuously attracted the attention of filmmakers and journalists, attempting to sketch this fringe of the migrant population in such a picturesque habitat. The scant information that they had managed to obtain encouraged me to pursue my research, thinking that my approach would gain the confidence of the residents. I did eventually, but it was a long, testing journey – on their and my behalf, as anthropological participant observation implies. To be part of the community is to understand its social functioning and structure (the etic approach), but also its conflict resolution, unsaid problems, discomforts, coping strategies and symbolism (the emic approach), which can only be achieved through mutual acceptance and trust. That is the cornerstone of any fieldwork, as well as being an open-ended epistemological and analytic dilemma since the inception of anthropology (Boas 1920; Malinowski 1922; Mead 2016; Barley 1986). The cosmopolitan role of the anthropologist, making 'small-scale worlds' universal and furthering the knowledge of 'part societies and cultures' (Werbner 2008: 54), always relies on the generosity of their respondents (ibid.: 63). The invasive nature of the media cannot take into account such generosity, nor the self-scrutiny implied by qualitative analysis. Only such a process is able to render human experiences and meaning-making intelligible. According to Kant, the faculty of judgement is that which enables bringing the particular to the universal, the detail to its category. It is this faculty that the anthropologist is asked to activate, in order to draw on the particulars 'located in social fields' (ibid.: 54) and transform experiences into case studies. For instance, my first job was to overcome my own barriers as a woman, and a white and non-Muslim one, to carry out fieldwork in a male, African, Muslim environment, something that was unheard of, or at least quite rare. The schema of observer and observed was not even an option, as the boundaries were already blurred: the residents had to know me before they could consent to my fieldwork.

The difficulty of being a researcher in an environment only attended by professionals is exemplified by the first reaction of aversion towards me: the residents did not see any interest in having me there, since I was not carrying out any practical work for them. Thus, I described my research as providing a way of sensitising the public on how West African migrants live in France, in order to show another face of Islam, contrary to that portrayed during the riots or after the terrorist attacks – that is, uniquely as a threat to public order and security. Perhaps Islam could also be seen as a medium through which Muslims express their lives, as their way of relating to both the world and the spiritual realm. I explained that my interest was purely a sociological one, since I was not affiliated to any media organisation or political party, and that my research was based in the UK. In the end, they started to appreciate my focus on Islam, something that nobody had attempted before. Previous work in the *foyers* had, in fact, probably following the Durkheimian school, addressed their social organisation, migratory trends and informal economy, with little consideration for their practice of Islam and well-being, which they felt was at the heart of their lives as Muslims and human beings.

The turning point happened after several weeks of my attendance there, as I still had to obtain formal recognition from the imam of Foyer93. M&S and the *délégué* had formally facilitated my entrance into the *foyer*, but not opened the way to the residents' trust in me. After a series of frustrating denials and missed appointments, I eventually wrote a letter to the imam, which was brought to him by Marabata[1] a man in his forties from Kayes. Marabata is of slave descent (see Chapter 4) and is expected to carry out what is needed, from menial jobs to delivering information to the residents in their rooms. I had to chase Marabata on many occasions before he agreed to give my letter to the imam. Then, after more time elapsed, the imam eventually let me know, through Marabata, that he was ready to receive me. The news ran quickly through Foyer93. From then onwards, people knew me as the one studying Islam in the *foyer*, one who was 'protected' by the imam himself. A veil of sorts had been placed over my head, concealing my otherwise dangerous youth, single status and outsider demeanour.

The Afrique Partenaire Service

The Afrique Partenaire Service (henceforth APS) is an association that works with migrants and for migrants' health rights in Paris. APS is one of the best known organisations on the ground, so much so that at public meetings on this subject it is generally either invited or is one of the organisers. APS aims at supporting migrants, whose social concerns are a consequence of their medical condition. Residency rights for medical reasons[2] or work-related illnesses – accidents, unsalubrious environments and so forth – are the most common issues that APS deals with. APS is run by a Malian woman in her fifties named Bintou. She is much respected in this milieu for her work, but also for her compassion and devotion to her clients, mostly young migrants who see her as a 'mother', as I have been told. Bintou works together with a French woman, who helps her with the administrative paperwork, and is said to speak all the languages of Africa. This is because she speaks Bambara and Wolof, currency languages spoken throughout West Africa, in addition to Soninké and French. Bintou used to volunteer as a translator in the Bichat hospital in the south of Paris for West African patients who could not speak French. The hospital has now endorsed her services, calling upon the association to help in such cases.

APS offers an advisory service for migrants settling down in Paris that is extremely varied and diversified. It organises HIV prevention sessions (in French, Soninké and Bambara) at the centre and in the *foyers* and facilitates access to treatment for undocumented migrants; it provides counselling for African patients; it networks with other associations in the territory during public forums, and invests in the intellectual strength of the association by periodically convening public debates with health professionals, social workers, academics and so forth, on issues concerning migrants' health and well-being (e.g. housing conditions and cultural barriers). Once, a renowned healer was invited, as he was passing through Paris for a brief visit. The interest of the talk was in the healer's vision, largely shared, that biomedicine and traditional medicine should ally. His talk was as much acclaimed by its attendees, both community members and professionals, as it was rare. Marabouts and healers, who are considered valuable by the community, do not generally live in Europe. In fact, they only visit their followers and clients abroad so that the latter can benefit from their *baraka* (البركة), the divine gift, which marabouts are thought to possess through their proximity to God (I will come back to this from Chapter 5 onwards).

APS is also involved in the social integration of the migrants' family members, mediating on their behalf with employers, schools and health institutions. In this respect, it has put in place a programme to help Muslim families 'get out of polygyny', for example; this is quite a controversial issue in France, and a very popular one with the anti-migration lobby, for whom Muslim migrants are impossible to integrate into the French social fabric because of the customs that Islam entails. Finally, APS is active in the media too, airing a programme on Radio Libertaire. The broadcast aims at sensitising the public, both the migrant community and the French one, on the theme of integration, in the belief that only intercommunity dialogue can be the premise to a constructive relationship. Likewise, APS is the curator of a website where the main African headlines are showcased in order to provide information, seemingly divergent from the official coverage. A space is also dedicated to culture, where fictional and academic work and press releases by African intellectuals are showcased.

I took part in several meetings at the APS central office, which operates as a drop-in centre. People attend to discuss their legal and medical situations, often after very long waits, since many usually turn up. These sessions also help scrutinise whether migrants' demands are defendable on medical grounds or if they should be directed elsewhere. The centre is open in the afternoons, three times a week. Everyone is listened to, so that to answer all the queries, sometimes Bintou has to book appointments beyond her working hours. Through APS, I could assess the extent of the networking potential of associations of this kind, which work unflinchingly to benefit the migrant population. Thanks to Bintou's connections, I could visit other *foyers* in Paris and get the sense that they replicate almost identically the organisation, sample community and, sadly, state of abandonment of Foyer93.

The overriding feeling among the clients of APS, predominantly West African migrants, is that intermediaries and initiatives that are born out of the community itself are more trustworthy. They think that either belonging to the community or having a history of migration can be grounds for better grappling with the difficulties that migrants face in France in relation to their health-seeking behaviour and the bureaucratic processes involved. However, notwithstanding the cultural and/ or linguistic barriers that West African patients encounter in French medical institutions (and not only there), which can be soothed by social workers like Bintou, outright discrimination persists unnoticed. An example is provided by Sargent's (2006: 45) study on the reproductive strategies of Muslim Malian women in Paris. The negotiation of identities that these women undergo while 'pursuing individual and family goals', often expressed through an Islamic idiom, is at odds with the constraints that the healthcare system imposes on them.[3]

GRDR

The Groupe de Recherches et de Réalisations pour le Développement Rural (GRDR) is an association that aims at reducing the social discrimination faced by the people living in the *foyers* by assessing their social marginality (e.g. exclusion, illegality), poor access to health and housing, and so forth, and by acting to redress it. Like APS, mentioned above, it liaises with social workers. GRDR is a stone's throw from Foyer93, where it runs its activities (among other *foyers*). Thus, it was not difficult for me to become aware of its existence and to get in contact with it.

Primarily, GRDR helps the residents solve their legal and bureaucratic issues, especially considering that many of them are illiterate and struggle with both the paperwork and dealing with the institutions. In parallel, GRDR organises health orientation programmes in the *foyers*, while twinning with both the region of Kayes, on a project that coordinates grassroots hospital support, and Senegal, where it has set up small health centres. In Paris, GRDR runs a drop-in centre in the area of Seine-Saint-Denis.

GRDR has observed a consistent pattern throughout the West African *foyers* whereby the residents overwhelmingly resort to traditional and herbal treatments when ill, and to medical treatment only at a critical stage. GRDR, like APS, would favour a process of inclusion of traditional practices into mainstream official medicine in France. So far, the only example of such rare complementarity can be found at the Dakar Fann Hospital in Senegal, where transcultural psychiatry merges with community-based therapy, as implemented by pioneering French psychiatrist Henri Collomb (1979, 1980). However, the idea that migrants in France might receive (psychiatric) therapy tailored for them is currently receiving strong criticism and resistance, so it is very likely that this will never be pursued (see Chapter 7).

The principle driving the work of GRDR is the amelioration of the social condition of the people in the *foyers*, as integral to the promotion of their health and well-being. A discourse of political and social responsibilities is thus evinced. The overcrowding and deplorable state of hygiene of the *foyers* seems to override any other problems, which often arise as a consequence. Noise and pollution respectively cause sleeping pattern disorders and a high risk of contagion from infectious diseases; incidences of tuberculosis, respiratory problems and dermatitis are all common and aggravated by the close contact between the residents, in the rooms and communal areas. This is why during the COVID-19 vaccination campaign, in view of the difficult care pathways of elderly migrant workers and their premature ageing, it was decided to consider these people a priority from the age of 60. Pre-vaccination consultations and vaccine injections are also free for the residents.[4]

However, undocumented migrants have no choice other than to live in the *foyers*, where, generally, their relatives have found them a place. This situation, which should be temporary, may be prolonged for years, often weakening the morale and health of the residents and degrading the environment further. Nonetheless, the residents' prime concern is not their health (or lack thereof) once housing and a job are provided. It only becomes an issue when their ability to work and live normally is hindered. Preventive measures are almost entirely overlooked, since the residents either ignore or are not able to access the institutional mechanisms that are in place. Both unemployed and working migrants do not avail themselves of the *mutuelle*, health insurance, as they do not find it cost effective. Undocumented migrants can avail themselves of the Aide Medical État (state medical help), but the eligibility criteria are hard to meet (e.g. declaration of address and employment, which most of the illegal migrants cannot provide) and the paperwork too onerous for them. Ultimately, only retired people may have a pension scheme that covers their healthcare, although very few are entitled, as their employment history is often discontinuous or undocumented.

GRDR emphasises another important point, which also matches my data. When, as a final recourse, migrants eventually seek medical help, they often do so with distrust for both French doctors and the treatment they suggest. Moreover, people in the *foyers* do not like discussing their health, sometimes even with their own roommates, and they feel guilty when they fall ill, as if they have failed their purpose and their families' expectations. Their social vulnerability puts them even further apart from the public system – institutional and medical. Some are afraid of being spotted by police surveillance while in the hospital, or that the medical consultation might be too expensive. Even those who are entitled to free check-ups do not often avail themselves of them, unless they are close to returning to their home country and are keen on making sure that all the required vaccines are completed. They also undergo these tests upon arrival from Africa, since tropical diseases such as yellow fever and malaria are endemic throughout the Senegal River basin.

Reckoning with orientalist epidemiological epistemes separating European and Muslim countries as different healthscapes, with the latter as the sickly body of the world (Varlik 2017), is the contention that there might be specific migrants' pathologies. GRDR clearly denies this, unless it is understood in the sense that people from endemic areas are as prone to be carriers of infectious diseases as anyone else travelling through them would be. Moreover, in France there is no epidemiology on an ethnic basis that might support this statement. In fact, notwithstanding the recent amendments, according to the 1978 law, no official records can be kept to survey ethnic or religious diversity, since this is regarded as a breach of one's freedom and privacy. The only exceptions are in relation to HIV/AIDS, in which case the nationality of the patient, and whether or not they are of foreign origin, is asked. Alioune, my respondent at GRDR, says:

> It's not because one is a migrant that [one] is more prone to illnesses, infective or otherwise. People of French nationality, living in precarious conditions of life, might be more vulnerable in respect of certain pathologies than other nationals, who are better off. If you see how people live in the *foyers*, if you see their insalubrious dwelling places, you then realise how their vul-

nerability affects their life and health: mental and physical. We face social determinants, more than specific pathologies related to specific groups. The relationship migration–health should be reframed in the context of the social environment. So, there aren't specific illnesses for particular groups, especially in France where patients are treated as a whole, regardless of their nationality or other specificities.

Crucially, at GRDR, I could see the breadth of the scope of activities that grassroots associations like these carry out, and how difficult it is for them to operate in such critical environments, often with little funding. Development projects outnumber those related to health (both in France and in the home country) because they produce revenue, whereas the latter are more costly and difficult to implement, requiring expensive equipment and more expert personnel. Development projects thus receive more attention and funding from the local municipalities, but also from NGOs looking for intermediaries with whom they can work. The focus on the migrants' home countries rather than on projects promoting their well-being in France points to the overall will to stop migration, in accordance with the European goal of 'zero migration', a dystopic delusion of this global era.

Finally, GRDR's view of the migrants' illness aetiology gave me an interesting key with which to analyse their malaise as a result of marginalisation, rather than a foregone fact happening in a vacuum. Good health certainly encompasses the functioning of bodily and mental faculties, but these can only be pitched against the wider social, political and environmental contexts of any given historical moment. In the *foyer*, I would therefore have to both unpack the complexity of these overlapping layers and shed light on the ways in which the residents may still have control over their lives in the face of squalid housing and exclusion.

AFAF

Associations created on the initiative of individuals, working on social and cultural programmes for migrants, are copious in Paris. They are often run by people of migrant descent or by migrants themselves. The boom of associations of this kind dates back to the 1981 law that, as noted, gave migrants the right to create them. Mostly located around the Seine-Saint-Denis Oval, they frequently run language courses and set up work induction programmes (e.g. for accountancy or writing), cultural events and social gatherings. The French Association of African and French Women (AFAF) is one such association. AFAF helps women from West Africa through the difficult process of settling in France.

I became interested in its work at a public forum that gathered different associations working for migrants. It was held to provide information about their work, but also to allow them to network. Bintou, also present, introduced me to the president of AFAF, to whom I explained the nature of my fieldwork in Paris. She invited me join the language course (French and Arabic) that they provided for their public, and so I did.

The president of AFAF was from Mali, while the administrator was a French woman. The recipients of AFAF's initiatives were illiterate women, mainly from rural areas of Kayes. A Tunisian woman taught French and basic Arabic through the scriptures (the Qur'an and laudatory prayers), which proved useful at Foyer93, while I read the suras with the imam. The course, like all of AFAF's activities, was funded by the local municipality, together with the participants' contributions, and was held in a school to the south of Paris. The association also organised recreational events such as the very successful *atelier de cuisine*, or cooking workshop, hosted in a school, where anyone could take it in turns to cook and to teach the others her best recipe. A festive meal would then be shared between the school staff and the locals. AFAF also provided free school support for children from the neighbourhood whose school performance was poor.

The classes were an occasion for me to learn Arabic too, while getting to know these women in a very lively and enthusiastic atmosphere. They were all married and had children, with the exception of a widow and a young lady who was unable to conceive. The latter two attended the classes rarely, until they stopped coming altogether. They enjoyed the sympathy of the others, but at the same time they suffered stigmatisation of their status. Discussions about God were mixed with discussions about goods. Sometimes the president improvised a little market with items she had been able to assemble, such as imitation jewellery, clothing material and aphrodisiac chewing gum. Alternatively, the distraction of children crying or running around entertained our unique class. The teacher had insisted that all of us keep a notebook filled with all the new exercises and prayers from the Qur'an that we had to learn by heart and then repeat in class. The lessons would normally pause for the mid-morning break, during which the youngest members prepared tea with biscuits or yogurt cake, and were expected to do the washing up. Towards the end of the course, it was my turn to provide breakfast for all the others: I had become part of the group, its age hierarchy and roles.

One of AFAF's most poignant meetings was held after an infamous fire at a run-down building, in which many migrants died (in summer 2005). The president talked to the members in French, until the emotional talk caused the linguistic medium to veer towards Bambara. A trembling and a deep sigh ran through the room while the death of a Senegalese woman and two of her young children was recounted and mourned (as they translated to me later on). The president knew the husband of the deceased and had organised the meeting to mobilise the others to help him. They decided to collect money for him and to provide clothes for the children who had survived. He had lost every- thing in the fire. In their spare time, these women also cooked for those migrants and their families who were camping in the street, waiting to obtain housing; they also brought toys for the children and other ame- nities. Among the homeless were also people from different *foyers* whom police raids had forced out without prior notice. Often, such prompt- ness to act was dictated by the otherwise almost complete lack of aid they would receive, meanwhile showing the great deal of social capital in these communities, which helped them survive through solidarity chains and interpersonal aid in times of hardship.

It has been argued (Quiminal and Timera 2002) that women seem to be more versatile than men, possibly because they are more embedded in society thanks to the parental care of their children – the school, leisure centres and other such places become gathering points and sites of social interaction. Upon migration, they progressively detach from both village life and the authority of elders and husbands. They grad- ually get into work and organising through female associations, which brings them out of the house and into contact with other possibilities. At Foyer93, I heard repeatedly that men opposed bringing their women to France, where 'they misbehave and become impolite', meaning that they acquire independence and make their own decisions. Nonetheless, young couples exhibit changing behaviour: husband and wife live to- gether in France, while limiting the size of their family – both in terms of children and the number of wives. It is argued that large families are unaffordable and very difficult to manage in France. Thus, the idea that Muslim families and women reproduce village sociocultural mod- els (polygyny and high fertility rates, most obviously) is misplaced. It reproduces a model from the colonial tradition, according to which women represent the way forward and those with whom the Republic can best maintain a dialogue (Wihtol de Wenden 1998), as opposed to their men, who would be backward, oriented towards village initiatives and only concerned with tradition and/or religion. Moreover, religious fervour as an indicator of poor social integration – with integration conceived of as secularism, proficiency in French, work and education, after Tribalat's (1995) definition – can be misleading. The Islamic ritual practice of fully integrated female Algerians and West Africans is more private than that of men, yet it is as strong as that of their counterparts, or stronger (Wihtol de Wenden 1998).

In conclusion, the social and medical aid provided to minority groups by associations run by or together with migrants is ample and well organised. Despite the enormous difficulties that (Muslim) migrant men and women alike face in France, it appears that they are ready to embrace them. This has intensified the formation of grassroots associations and inter-aid forms of solidarity, which provide constant reference points for the community. In times of crisis, they are the first to mobilise. Unfortunately, the lives of these associations are often short-lived, due to budgetary cuts and a political climate that thwarts the accommodation of minority groups in France, especially when they are Muslim. Revenue-making development projects that consolidate a stronger French presence in Africa are favoured in their lieu.

Notes

1. Out of respect for my respondents' anonymity and safety, the names provided henceforth are pseudonyms.
2. This was true only for treatments not available in the patients' home countries. Since 2010, health provision has been extended to benefit all those who have been living in France for at least a year.
3. Malian women are always given prescriptions for contraceptive pills: although the phenomenon of repeated pregnancies is certainly dangerous for these mothers, it also impinges on the cost of the French welfare system.
4. See https://solidarites-sante.gouv.fr/grands-dossiers/vaccin-covid-19/je-suis-un-pro fessionnel-de-sante-du-medico-social-et-du-social/article/supports-d-informa tion-diffusables-pour-les-travailleurs-migrants-en-foyer (accessed 17 March 2022).

3

A *Foyer* as a Home

Once Upon a Time, the Soninkés

Soninké society is segmentary, that is, it is divided by clan rivalries for the acquisition of power and based on control over family lands. Families in turn are also productive units, or *ka*, made of different households of the same lineage (Pollet and Winter 1971; Manchuelle 1997; Timera 1996). Each family head, the *ka gumme* or leader of the *ka*, is the oldest member of the lineage, which branches into different households, each contributing to the wealth of the *ka*. The organisation of work is distributed between the main field, where the *ka gumme* works with the help of his sons for the main part of the day, and the individual plot, the *saluma*, in which various people work for the rest of the day. Women also work their lands to supplement with side ingredients (such as peanuts) the main food items (such as cereals), which are provided by the men of the *ka* (Manchuelle 1997: 31), In the past, work in the fields was carried out mainly by slaves, which were also the currency of exchange with which to obtain goods or help during migration along the caravan routes in the desert or in the southern regions (ibid.).

Bureaucratic apparatuses traditionally remain very elementary, even when the state is in place, and it is the royal clan and its clients who ensure that it functions effectively. In non-state societies, the royal clan constitutes a greater number of lineages in competition for power. When a clan manages to impose itself over the others, the state mode is then brought to bear again. This applied to the Soninkés up until the nineteenth century, when the royal clans exerted two forms of power: the *laada* and the *jonghu*. The first meant that clients (the griots, singers of the family epic; the *forgerons*, iron-makers who were and still are also responsible for carrying out circumcision; and the marabouts or clerics) participated in the royal family rituals. The second was an oath that bound families to protect each other. Royal families were not the only ones to have clients attached to them: the nobles had their clerics (the marabouts), caste families and slaves (ibid).

Competition for power is the mark of segmented societies, where the land is the main source of wealth and the founding element of a lineage, since through its distribution and productivity families can live and establish their households. For Manchuelle, building a clientele was central to this endeavour and was only possible through 'generosity and prestige' (1997: 19), both made possible by wealth and 'generalised exchange, such as favours, intermarriage and gifts' (ibid.: 17). In the Senegal River Valley, wealth was provided by agriculture and by 'seasonal trading expeditions' (ibid.: 14). The Soninkés were the first *julas*, itinerant merchants of West Africa. This insight undermines both the colonial idea of an African subsistence economy in the region and the notion of migration as the result of uprooting. The Soninké empire lasted from the twelfth century until the eighteenth. In the nineteenth century they were restricted to forming segmentary states with independent villages and towns under the rule of important clans. By then, the Soninkés were surrounded by the powerful Bambara and Bidan people, although their economic viability in the region remained unchanged (ibid.).

The relative stability of the central state authority emphasised in turn the internal political organisation of the villages, through hierarchical family power structures. The village, like the kingdom, was also segmentary, such that internal rivalries for power endured, with younger members aspiring to overturn the leader, generally the oldest in the village (Manchuelle 1997: 19). The chief of the village had his cohort of elders, who in more recent terms are defined as 'the sages'. Villages tended to be socially homogenous, with one dominating social group. Thus, one could find royal villages, maraboutic ones, villages of artisans and so on. Warriors headed the marabouts' villages, since marabouts could not head them themselves (ibid.). Notwithstanding that such hierarchies have formally disappeared in what is now the Republic of Mali, the village structure remains true to traditional custom, even upon migration (see following chapter).

Migration has historically been at the nexus of the French Republic, especially during the Wars of Algeria and Indochina, when many

French people were recruited to the army and a million Algerians returned home to fight for Algerian Independence. The industrial demand for migrant labour peaked, so that migration became structural to the French economy. It was officially processed through the Office National de l'Immigration (ONI), which then became the Office de Migrations Internationales (OMI), and migrants from North and West Africa were welcomed. It was not long before it all went sour: French public housing (as seen above) could not match the exorbitant demands placed upon it, so most of the migrants turned to the *cités*, to unhealthy squats and to the *foyers* to survive.

The first *foyers* were provided by the patronage of the industries as facilities for French internal migrants. The *foyers* called SONACOTRAL (Societé National de Construction pour les Travailleurs Algerians, 1955–70), housing Algerian migrants, soon followed. They were managed by the Ministry of the Interior, which could thus supervise the Algerian migrants. These were the years of the Algerian War of Independence, when the *foyers* resembled a military base more than they did public housing. Memory of this can still be found, as those *foyers* are still standing: the rooms are built around a central space, meant to be occupied by a controller or guard, who had to identify the residents. Directors of these types of *foyers* were generally ex-combatants, or people with a military career and training.

In time, responding to the changed historical context, these *foyers* went on to include all workers, beyond the Algerians, and to be known as '*foyers* SONACOTRA'. SONACOTRA would later manage and sponsor the creation of new *foyers* out of old factories. Associations like the Association pour la Formation Technique de base des Africains et Malgaches (AFTAM) and the Soutien Union Dignité Accueil du Travailleur Africain (SOUNDIATA) arose as managing associations of the *foyers* under the Ministry of Cooperation and Education, while their Administrative Council shares its functions with the migrants' representatives. This gives them a less rigid approach in contrast to the SONACOTRA *foyers*, whereby a degree of self-management is endorsed (Fievet 1999).

The *foyers* appear to be largely an independent microcosm. They are spread out across the whole Île-de-France region, and to a certain extent, they do not constitute a novelty in the established social scenario. Nevertheless, they remain foreign to the reality of most French people, who are not directly involved with them (see Chapter 2). Seine-Saint-Denis, located to the north-east of Paris, is one of the smallest *départments*[1] of the Île-de-France region and one of the three banlieues encircling Paris. This *département* is commonly referred to as the 'neuf-trois' (the 'nine-three'), in reference to its postcode. According to the 1999 census, the 'neuf-trois' has the highest number of migrants in the whole region (21.7 per cent, of which 17.3 per cent are from non-EU countries), with the highest mortality and unemployment numbers compared to national rates (respectively 5.7 per thousand and 13.5 per cent). In 2018, it was estimated that up to 20 per cent of the population in the *department* were illegal migrants (Leclerc 2018). Its location in the 'neuf-trois' is also the reason for 'Foyer93' as the symbolic name for my field site.

A former SONACOTRAL *foyer*, Foyer93 is now run and owned by AFTAM. Associations like the above-mentioned GRDR and the Collectif pour l'Avenir des Foyers (COPAF, founded in 1996) mediate between AFTAM and the residents. Foyer93 is one of the most populous and best-known *foyers* in Montreuil. It was converted from a piano factory some fifty years ago. The majority of its residents come from Mali.

What follows is a fairly 'thick description' of the environment of Foyer93, provided in order to explain how the residents have made it their own.

The women who work at the canteen are often from Mali, and in particular from the villages of origin of the residents themselves. They apply to the Residents Committee, which recruits them on the basis of their skills. These can be bolstered by previous experience developed in other *foyers* or school canteens, cultural centres and so forth in Paris. It is also not unlikely that they might know someone at Foyer93 who facilitate the process. They work in shifts for periods of six months. Their wage is provided by the day's takings, after the money used to buy the food is deducted. The cooks also pay a small fee for the use of the facilities, which goes towards the savings of the *foyer*. The state of the canteen, like that of the rest of Foyer93, is abysmal. Food lies everywhere, and there are no refrigerators. As soon as one enters Foyer93, one can see, beyond the huge dump right in the middle of the court, sacks of potatoes, onions and carrots on the edges of the perimeter walls next to the canteen. This would not be a problem in itself if food could be washed properly, which is not the case, since there is just a small sink and food is put in plastic or aluminium calabashes, which are also left lying about in the kitchen, where cockroaches and rats sneak in.

Foyer93 is infested with rats; they have even eroded the wires and pipes of the canteen, so that illumination can be intermittent and the risk of gas leaks is always present. This subject has often been brought to the attention of the consultation council of the *foyer*, with which I sat on many occasions, yet the solutions that AFTAM has suggested, in accordance with COPAF, have not met the residents' agreement. The former encourages changes to sanitise the canteen and bring it to the standard norm: it would buy fridges in which the food could be stored, renovate the whole place and demand that the *cuisinières* (the cooks) attend safety and hygiene training, while implementing standard procedures (e.g. the use of gloves and detergents, and the cleaning of the working areas). The standardisation of the *cantine sociale*, a 'soup kitchen' of sorts, would also grant the workers the status of fully fledged employees, with fixed wages and sickness and accident cover.

The residents oppose this plan, not so much to protect some of the workers, who are illegal or in the process of gaining legal status, but because it might change the dynamics of Foyer93 considerably. For instance, a formally run canteen would bring third parties into the *foyer*, and these would be interlocutors with whom the residents would have to deal and over whom they feel they have no decisive power. The relationship of the residents with AFTAM is one of opposition, even though it dates back to the 1960s. The residents feel that AFTAM interferes with the way that they want to organise the *foyer*, for instance by its constant demands for rent increases to ameliorate the *foyer*. Moreover, changes in the management of the canteen would imply a rise in the cost of the meals, from the very basic €2–3.50 to at least €4–5. On a daily basis, this price would of course have to be doubled, based on the consumption of lunch and supper, without breakfast (although some also have breakfast at Foyer93 before leaving for work).

The residents generally share a midsized or large calabash in groups of two or three with their fellow roommates, which further reduces the price of the whole meal for everyone. The standardi ation of the canteen would imply the elimination of such practices altogether, through the introduction of individual plates and the directive to consume food on the premises of the canteen. This would impact on their finances by costing them almost as much as eating elsewhere in Paris, contradicting the status of the *foyers* as *résidences sociales* (social housing). Once all of the residents' resources were spent in affording them a life in Paris, their roles as family providers would be hindered and their migration projects would fail. So far, no implementation plan has been approved: a status quo is maintained that goes hand in hand with the advanced deterioration of Foyer93.

The residents' denial about their dejected lifestyle is overt and can only make sense in the bigger picture of their individual trajectories. Once at Foyer93, they have already endured the ordeal of the journey to Europe, the difficulties of gaining access to Foyer93 and of obtaining the right to a bed. They have established a routine with their fellow residents; they have become accustomed to the rhythm of the big city

(Kleinman 2019), to the gruelling working schedule if they have a job (generally menial work) or to the humiliating quest for temporary jobs, which is a constant feature of their lifetime in Paris. Some of them scrape a living with petty jobs and activities set up on their own initiative in the *foyers* around Paris or in Barbès, an up-and-coming district in the eighteenth arrondissement of Paris, where they sell phone cards or other merchandise acquired through illegal networks. In this neighbourhood, recently opened art shops, bookshops, small ethnic restaurants and nightclubs attract both the locals, mainly of Western and North African origin, and the bohemian glitterati of Paris, who enjoy the rich cultural mix of this part of town.

The invisibility of the *foyer* residents in Paris is their only way to counter the fear of being expelled, of working without a permit. The unhygienic conditions of Foyer93 are, if anything and quite emblematically, the least of their preoccupations. Only on occasions of celebrations (Muslim or otherwise) and during the preparations for their return home do they allow themselves more visibility. This is when they spend more time aiming to be seen and greeted, talking to the other residents about their imminent departure, as well as to gather pictures and letters from their friends, which they will deliver to their respective families in the villages. Otherwise, the normality at Foyer93 is one in which life passes by in anonymity: the risk that fights may erupt is always around the corner, so the residents keep themselves to themselves. This is why those who can share their rooms with family members are privileged: they can trust each other and have a token family life.

At Foyer93, the tailoring workshop is a very small barrack in the main court, just opposite the dump. It contains all the paraphernalia useful in a workshop of this kind, including sewing machines and a working area made up of a table (the limited space does not allow for more than one person inside at a time). Rolls and pieces of fabric lie about and are entangled with the wires that provide electricity for both the scant lighting and the machines. A couple of chairs complete the sparse furnishing. The workers at the tailor's workshop, like those at the cafeteria and at the canteen, take it in turns to work for periods of a few months, so that the chance to gain a secure wage is given to the largest possible number of people. Working at Foyer93 is a very sought-after opportunity. People feel safer here than anywhere else, whether they are documented migrants or not. They have their own pace of work, as opposed to one that an employer would impose on them. Although their schedule is relentless and around the clock, they do not feel exploited, as they would in other menial jobs. They work thanks to and for the community, fulfilling needs that they perceive would otherwise remain unsatisfied. Where would they go to commission the making of a traditional gown in Paris? How much would it cost? How would they be looked upon while making their requests? The 'ethnicisation' of minority groups may indeed be construed as the process by which the former seek to conform to the Republican project without ever really succeeding, thereby withdrawing into their own communities (Fall 2005).

A variety of residents and customers from outside Foyer93 make use of the workshop both to stitch up their garments and to make new ones, be they in Western or traditional fashion. It is worth noting that in the same way that the preparation of food is a highly gendered occupation in this milieu (and in Southern Europe too!) and exclusively a female one, tailoring is reserved for men. The acquisition of the machines entails the business capacity to buy them, which is not granted to most Malian women in Paris, although in the region of Kayes, women work in the fields and in the maintenance of their homesteads. When they engage in business activities, these are essentially the sale of food and gadgets at market stands, often set up through the money sent by a family member abroad (a husband or brother). Throughout Paris, tailors' shops also respect this gender division, while of course, the clientele is diversified. In the numerous workshops of traditional garments in Barbès, people work in groups of six or more at their sewing machines, very much like a conveyer belt in industrial production (another gendered workplace). The consultation council has gathered on different occasions to discuss measures to sanitise and prevent fire hazards at Foyer93, including the workshop. These issues evoked the incontrovertible constraints of class described by Orwell (1989), rendered in the image of a woman fiddling with a stick in a pipe outside her house, clogged by sewage. The workshop was kept open throughout the time of my fieldwork, only to be shut recently. It has not been replaced by anything else, nor has any proposition been advanced.

Traditional rules regulating the relationship between the elders and the youth – the *cadets* – are somewhat reversed at Foyer93, where status and seniority take precedence. Those who arrived first retain seniority rights vis-à-vis those who arrived later. This is motivated by at least two reasons. The first is that there is not space for newcomers. They can only hope to sleep in the already overcrowded rooms, sharing the rent (if they can), grateful to be offered this opportunity. The second is that the only possibility for replacing someone comes when a resident vacates a bed for months or for good. In order to avoid disputes and given the long waiting list, the person with the right to the bed decides who will occupy it. Replacements are carried out very quickly and often without AFTAM knowing.

As a woman carrying out research at Foyer93, I was advised not to stay there after dark, so I relied on my respondents' accounts to collect data about the nightlife in the *foyer*, which seemingly undergoes a transformation, becoming a huge dormitory. The number of people who sleep on the floor is almost double the number of those who are entitled to a bed. The former sleep wherever possible: in the corridors and in the canteen. Mattresses are laid out towards the evening, which signalled the time for me to leave. In addition, as testified by M&S (Migrations et Santé 2003), 10 per cent of the residents resort to prostitution. According to my respondent Kane, 32 and from Tambakara, this is performed in the toilets by female prostitutes.

In the scenario in which the community is fragmented into smaller *foyers* and professional workers introduced, the jobs currently carried out in a traditional way among community members will be lost. The residents do not look backwards or suffer from an over-attachment to the lives that they used to live in Kayes per se. Simply, and more crucially, the community that has so far granted their first entry into France and their ongoing support in Paris would be weakened and dispersed. This niche provides the migrant with a series of opportunities, both in and outside the *foyer*, such that the possibility of staying in Paris indefinitely becomes real. As long as they can send their remittances home, and thus contribute to the wealth of their homeland, their absence from Kayes is justified. More importantly, their migratory project has succeeded. The migrant can now find a place in the community that does not simply correspond to their place in the village, but also to their community in Paris, giving them a new status, protection and economic leverage of a kind.

Among the residents, together with a discourse about their sentimental attachment to the village, another has burgeoned, revealing their intention to embrace life in Paris, where they intend to work and build meaningful relationships. What keeps this project viable is their own community of people, who share their daily constraints and suffering with them. For young and not so young, rural, often undocumented migrants, a migratory project to France would be impossible without intracommunity aid and networking: they would lack both the cultural and social capital on which to build their existence in France. The economic drive that has brought so many from Kayes to France is increasingly being transformed into a subjective one. New ideas of prestige are eclipsing the dream of the successful migrant returning home, such that this is now more a Republican wish than a reality on the ground.

The Residents

The capacity of Foyer93 is 1,035 beds, but the delegate representing its members at the Residents Committee (I will come to this later) estimates that there are around 2,250 residents in the foyer, since those who have the right to a bed (generally documented migrants) guarantee hospitality to their family members or fellow villagers. Illegal migrants may over time acquire legal status and thus the right to a bed, so they will eventually help other family members as they have been helped. The solidarity chain ensures not simply the migratory cycle, but most of all the community's survival. People who have lost family and/or community links, or have come to France without any contacts, usually encounter many more difficulties than the others.

Salif, for example, a man in his thirties from Kayes, was found by M&S, sleeping outside Foyer93 on pieces of cardboard in autumn. Given the scant relevance of people's legal status with respect to accessing Foyer93, I wondered how this might have occurred. The answer was that Salif had no connections with any of the residents. He was not even allowed to sleep on the floor of the canteen or in the corridors, which were already crammed with people at night. It was only through the intervention of M&S that Salif was eventually given a place on the ground floor, although he was left alone and barely greeted by the others at the cafeteria or other communal areas. This explains the high recurrence of people from the same areas, if not the same village. Unsurprisingly, the survey provided by M&S on the nationalities present at Foyer93 confirms that the majority are Malians, followed by Mauritanians, people with acquired French nationality, Senegalese, Burkinabe, Central African and finally Ivorian residents. Malian residents come predominantly from the administrative subdivisions (or *cercles* in French) of Kayes and Yelimané. Each *cercle* includes a number of smaller towns, communes and villages, which I present in the following table, according to their representation at Foyer93 in decreasing order.

According to M&S's report, 59 per cent of people come from rural villages areas (as mentioned above) and 74 per cent of these are aged between 25 and 45; 44 per cent are married, against 52.5 per cent who are single; 49 per cent have children, of which 96 per cent live in Mali. Because of their illegal status, 64 per cent of the residents do not go back to Mali, while 13 per cent can only once every two years. Even those who have a job wait a long time to take a holiday, since when they return to Mali, they spend at least two months there. Moreover, the cost of the flight and the financial expectations of the family weigh a lot on the migrants' budgets. The Muslim principle of *sadaqah* (صدقة), donation,

Table 3.1. Villages represented at Foyer93. © D. Accoroni.

Highest percentage	Kayes *cercle*	Yelimané *cercle*
1	Kayes Capital city of the *cercle*	
2	Commune of Segalà	
3	Commune of Kabaté	
4	Commune of Sadiolà	
5		Commune of Guidimé
6		Town of Yelimané
7		Commune of Dafounou Gory
8		Village of Gory Sambaga
9		Village of Tambakara
10		Village of Konsiga
11		Town of Kersiniané
12		Commune of Toya
13		Village of Yaguiné

becomes an imperative for them, since their families believe and are made to believe that in Europe, everyone is at ease, that money is available for all. Migrants are expected to bring presents and to give money to family and friends who come and visit them. They are supposed to pay for the cost of medications, family celebrations (births, funerals, weddings and so on) and Muslim celebrations if these take place when they are there (e.g. *eïd-al-kabir* [عيد الكبير], *eïd-al-fitr* [عيد الفطر] and throughout the sacred month of Ramadan). Furthermore, they may be asked to contribute in some way to local development through the associations they may be part of, or by investing in family possessions (e.g. brick houses and other constructions). The preparation for the journey home is literally a family business and a sign of success, and therefore is all the more thought through.

Finally, 80.3 per cent of the residents have a good command of French, but only 55 per cent can write it. The languages normally spoken are Bambara and Soninké, even by those from Central Africa or Ivory Coast, due to previous contacts in Africa through internal migration. The scenario that opens up to the researcher is one that suggests an extremely ghettoised lifestyle, taking place in crammed and claustrophobic rooms or dormitories, with little contact with the external world. Only 28 per cent of them work officially, yet many more have interim jobs or do not have authorisation to work. Undeclared labour will eventually become a problem during their retirement, when they risk being excluded from pension schemes, even if they have been working for more than twenty years in France.

The residents' ages range from 18 to over 65, but young boys do come to France before reaching adulthood (personal communication). I found that a series of denials are mobilised by the residents to protect themselves from French law concerning their legal status, religious practices, marriage relationships and so forth. At a very early stage of my fieldwork, it seemed that no one ever saw a marabout; minors did not migrate; migrants' wives were all in the home country; the migrants' illegal status got sorted out at some point; peace and harmony reigned at Foyer93; and Islam was the means by which all this was achieved. To an extent, these appearances concealed the residents' most intimate problems and their ways of dealing with them in settling down in Paris. In turn, polygyny, illegal migration and Islam were put forward by the French intelligentsia, and still are, as reasons for the failed integration of people like the residents of the *foyers* into French secular society. Secularism had become the battleground on which the different parties articulated their motivations respectively for refusing the Muslims as legitimate citizens and for pursuing such citizenship. The universal message of Islam paradoxically counters the universality of the French Republic, all the while deepening the divide between the two. However, the residents' concerns go well beyond their being Muslims in France, as I was told by Jibril, a man from Gory in his fifties: 'What really bothers us is being illegal; it's living in a place like this [Foyer93], always being short of money and not having a life!'

Management and Representation at Foyer93

The 2000 Solidarité et Renouvellement Urbain (Solidarity and Urban Renewal) Law was the outcome of a national deliberation on the improvement of housing and transport in France. It acknowledged that the living expectations and urban design of fifty years ago no longer corresponded to the current situation. The density of the population has increased and its concentration in the banlieues and in particular urban sectors, together with its isolation, has meant that in cities such as Paris, these have become hotbeds of degradation and social discontent. The *foyers* are among these places. Scattered within and outside Paris, they are a concern for the mayor of Paris; for managing associations like

AFTAM, ADOMA and ADEF (both ex-SONACOTRA, they were funded in the 1950s) and for those associations working within the *foyers*, such as COPAF at Foyer93. The law, at least in its intent, wished to promote urban and social diversity and to ease circulation by addressing urban congestion, poor housing and transportation. It also aimed at favouring 'sustainable development', firstly by solving the problem of overcrowding through a rational distribution of the population; secondly by safeguarding the rights of both buyers and residents; and finally, by improving transport links between the town and the periphery. For the first time ever, the *foyers* have also been sanctioned, while the people living there have come to be viewed as holding a 'special status', that is, as migrants living in social housing with the right to manage it as residents. Thus, this law gave legitimacy both to the Residents Committee (henceforth RC) and its Consultation Council (henceforth CC).

The RC represents the residents of the *foyers* in their negotiations with AFTAM, the managing body and owner of Foyer93, about everything concerning the organisation, expenses and communal life in the *foyer*, as well as its internal cohesion. The RC has the right to defend their interests in any legal procedure, including litigations with AFTAM, and the right to sanction the entry of third parties into the *foyer* (e.g. cultural associations and professionals). RC members are elected, and each managing association chooses its electoral system. The most democratic one is by list, as opposed to the less representative self-candidature system. AFTAM follows the first, while others, such as ADEF, have adopted the second. Only the RC can nominate its representatives for the CC, chosen proportionally from the majority lists, and eventually for a larger committee coordinating different RCs. RC representatives, up to ten, nominate their president, secretary and treasurer. Elections are carried out through an Electoral Commission made up of RC members, third parties such as the mayor or their representatives, and associations working for the *foyers*, whose number cannot exceed that of the *délégués* sitting on the RC (therefore, not more than ten at Foyer93). The president of the Electoral Commission guarantees the smooth running of elections and their budget. As COPAF maintains, the importance of other parties in the Electoral Commission is that the elected RC becomes more visible externally (vis-à-vis the borough, for instance), while more transparency is granted internally. Interestingly, when the RC is not in place, the residents' representatives in the Electoral Commission are provided by the *Comité des Sages*, the Committee of the Wise Men.

The 'Wise Men' are the highest expression of traditional organisation in the *foyers*. They are the elders, whose opinion is sought over controversies in cases where the *délégués* or other ranked men – such as the imam and the marabout – have not found a solution. It is worth noting that in the most run-down *foyers*, the village and traditional structure is much stronger than in the most modern ones. The so-called *foyers-taudis* or hovel *foyers* are the older ones, usually huge buildings with large rooms, in which a logic of 'community access', as practised at Foyer93, is possible. Smaller and newly restored *foyers* are conceived with the aim of housing migrants from different countries and of having rooms that can host three people at most. Community organisation is hindered here, and a market logic is applied. Rent is nearer to the market price and the relationship between managing association and residents is closer to that between owner and lodger. Thus, they are trapped between hammer and anvil. They can hope to achieve better living conditions at higher prices, while dispersing the community and being much more exposed and controlled; or remain in the *foyers-taudis* until their legal situation is cleared, while their number and self-organisation protects them. The choice is impossible – also in the sense that they have no choice.

RC candidates must have resided for at least three months in the *foyer* and have the right to a bed – that is, be fully fledged residents. Their mandate lasts three years and can be renewed – another element testifying to the long periods of residence in the *foyers*, contrary to the idea of fast turnovers. Currently, however, young people move out of the *foyers* more quickly than those in their thirties and older, whose responsibilities have grown with the number of family members they have to provide for (e.g. children, wives, old parents and the extended family), and whose migration followed a different family path and work project.

'[The] CC is the permanent organ of dialogue and consultation between the residents, the managing association and the owner, if this is different from the managing association.'[2] The CC is consulted for any matter concerning the *foyers*, from the life of its people to its physical space. Once a year, the managing association must present a budgetary report to the CC, giving an account of the expenses incurred during the year and those expected for the next. The majority of the CC must vote in order to issue decisions or changes. In cases of dissent, the proposition has to be voted on a second time. If it is rejected again, the proposition will not pass. The proposed projects in the canteen that have stalled for years are an example.

The CC should convene at least every two to three months, and the RC can demand the presence of an administrator of AFTAM, according to the agenda. The latter, except for urgent matters, should be communicated before the meetings, during which a secretary is designated to take the minutes. Topics touched on during the meetings range from concerns regarding ordinary matters of maintenance to the overcrowding of the corridors and public areas or the pressing relocation plan to move the residents into a new *foyer* in the area, whose construction is underway. On many occasions, the positions of AFTAM and of the RC, which is generally supported by COPAF, diverge. The points of disagreement bring to the fore the stakes involved in both community-making and management, especially when the power relations are unbalanced.

AFTAM is an association that was founded in 1962 with the purpose of helping migrants from the ex-colonies find accommodation in Paris and integrate into French society. It also promotes development projects with the active participation of the residents of the AFTAM *foyers*, such as Foyer93, as well as professional induction. During 1964–65, AFTAM became involved in the acquisition and transformation of ex-factories into *foyers* and dormitories. By the 1980s, AFTAM had delivered professional and language classes totalling seven hundred thousand hours; in 2000, it launched a project called Projet d'Entreprise Associative (Social Business Project), networking with other entities in Paris and the Île-de-France region to implement co-development in Africa. Since 1999, AFTAM began the renovation of a third of its *foyers* into social residences, housing about three to four hundred people, in cooperation with the mayor of Paris. AFTAM now has the status of a social enterprise, in that its beneficiaries are the general public in need, and thus not exclusively the residents of the *foyers*. The idea is that the latter will eventually move into smaller, more compact and more expensive housing. Migrants are considered less and less to be disadvantaged people needing social aid, so that the shift from the *foyers-taudis* to market housing is envisaged, together with the closure of Foyer93 and similar *foyers*.[3]

It is no wonder that the projects of renovation suggested by AFTAM do not meet the residents' favour. This is a conflict point, which the residents, through their representatives who sit in the CC meetings, vote down at any occasion. After the meetings, the delegates have to explain the outcomes and proceedings of the consultations to the residents. At these times, the whole of Foyer93 vibrates with news. The delegates have a great responsibility, since they are the repository of the residents' will, which is not undivided. The president of the RC, Mamadou, not only fears that decisions by the CC may not favour them, he has to respect the existing customary hierarchies, often at odds with the ambitions for social promotion and change of the younger residents. Although there is a large consensus to maintain Foyer93 as it is, some of the younger residents do not dismiss the possibility of minor changes, such as the introduction of an internet station, about which the elders are not too concerned. Thus, AFTAM has suggested the installation of an internet connection in the meeting room, where formal meetings and language classes are held; if this were to pass, it would obviously create a problematic overlap.

Until the end of my fieldwork, the computer facilities had not been put in place. What is available for the residents is only a public telephone in the cafeteria, where barely two people can stand at once, and which is open during the day throughout the week. In this way, they can make calls as they would in phone centres, without having to go to the nearest one outside Foyer93.[4] The charges are established by AFTAM, while the takings are used to pay those who supervise the service. The relationship between AFTAM and the residents is one of ongoing battle that only allows for minor changes, if any at all.

Notes

1. In French, the *département* is the administrative division of a region. The *banlieues* stand generally for them, as they have a wider meaning than 'outskirts of a town' or 'suburbs'. They comprise the departments surrounding the capital city of a region and including smaller communes.
2. See: Bill on the Election of the Members in the RC and CC, SRU 2000 Law, Article 3, L 633-4-3.
3. As of 2018, of the 687 households identified in 1997, housing 100,000 workers, 437 have been renovated, 87 have been closed and 163 are awaiting treatment, as reported by the Interministerial Commission for The Housing of Immigrant Populations (Cilpi), responsible for piloting the renovation. See Duriez (n.d.).
4. With the introduction of smartphones, the service has lost much of its use, although a landline always has the advantage of providing both a means of communication to those who do not have a phone or have lost it, and a domicile number when administrative procedures demand it.

4

Caste, Class and Gender at Foyer93

Society and People

In (West) Africa, family names bear witness to former caste affiliations, which are partially still present in Soninké society. The Soninké ethnic group is part of the larger Mande population, descendants of the Empire of Ghana, or Wagadou Empire (750–1240). They 'formed a principal element in Ghana, namely a class of court functionaries and administrators. Their family names (Sylla, Doukouré, Niakhate, Nimaga and Konaté) and titles can be found unchanged among the Soninkés …. The Mandes gave rise to the Mandé-Jola and Marka people, who migrated from Wagadou during the decline of Mali'; it seems that the 'Soninké clans, specialized in trade, Islamic scholarship and law, migrated instead into the Malian provinces … and further East and South' (Massing 2000: 288–89). The Soninké Wangaras, traders of gold and salt at the time of the great trans-Saharan trade, can be identified with the Malinkés, princes and warriors (ibid.: 287). The Empire of Mali (1230–1600) was founded by Soundiata Keita (1217–55), a Malinké, whose epic is sung by the griots, bards who chant the praises of Soundiata's empire and who are still the repositories of the oral tradition.

At Foyer93, the residents can be heard intercalate their surnames with salutations upon greetings others in acknowledgement of their respective family ancestries. There can be either pride or shame according to the family's status. An example of the former is the following exchange between a Doukouré and a Koli, both functionaries' surnames:

K: Ah Doukouré! How are you?
D: Koli, everything's fine and you?
K: Fine. And the family?
D: Good, thanks God – and work?
K: Busy, busy. I'm a bit tired, but fine!
D: OK, Koli, see you soon
K: Doukouré, see you soon.[1]

People like Marabata, of slave descent, bear witness to the eclectic negotiation of traditional values and pragmatic needs, marking the passage
between one society and the next, or rather, from the homeland to the
diaspora. In traditional Soninké society, the slaves would have been part
of the family units in which they worked and lived. Slaves served as a
manual labour force bound to carry out menial jobs as the household
required. At Foyer93, Marabata is known as 'the slave'. He is in his late
forties and is from Tambakara. He is not supposed to hold paid work,
since his role is that of serving the community; therefore, he is granted
free meals at the canteen and pocket money for his personal needs. Like
many others, he spends most of his time at Foyer93 and in the neighbourhood. He often supports the delegates in coordinating and carrying
out cleaning jobs in the *foyer* and in unloading deliveries, finding people and delivering news. If the delegates are the official representatives,
Marabata is a further interface, the informal and yet vital intermediary
to get into the community at Foyer93. When the delegates or the imam
are absent, nobody will speak to you unless Marabata has somehow introduced you to the residents, showed you around the *foyer* and most
fundamentally, accepted your query. Marabata and I have become friends
over time. He would share jokes with me and offer me (soft) drinks at
the cafeteria. He is an undocumented migrant, but a senior resident of
Foyer93 too. Because of his role in the *foyer* and the support he receives
from the residents, he has gained a higher reputation within the community than he would have at Tambakara. One resident told me about him:
 'He is good. He is one of the few who do something useful here! He
really helps and works hard.'
 Marabata also enjoys the privilege of living with other senior residents
on the third and uppermost floor of Foyer93, and therefore of having a
landline in his room. The rooms on the upper floors are slightly quieter,
since they are further away from the hubbub of the court, although people pour into the corridors at night, including those of the upper floors.
Marabata never went back to Kayes during the whole period of my fieldwork, nor was he planning to. He would inform me of all the comings
and goings of the others as if they did not concern him. One could argue
that Marabata is quite emblematically the modern face of slavery.

The griots add to the social composition of Soninké society. They used to, and still do, chant the epic of Soundiata and the genealogy of the aristocracy by heart or by way of improvisation. They are able to memorise complex kinship relationships and their related anecdotes, mixing reality with fantasy in a fictional, semi-historical representation of the facts. At Foyer93, Diana was one such griot. He was no longer a resident of the *foyer*, but he still came for visits over weekends and spent a good deal of time in the court and the cafeteria. Once, he even started a little chanting praise for me, until Makalou interrupted him – it was not rare that residents felt jealous of other residents' skills and status and attempted to undermine their position by way of mockery or, as in this case, by silencing them. A griot would have been attached to one important family, whose praises he would sing, receiving money for his services. However, the griots are no longer affiliated with renowned families as their patrons, but still sing during public celebrations, in Europe as much as in the homeland. They receive donations because of their role in the community and enjoy much appreciation and affection. Doukouré, one of the delegates, would say about them:

> The griots have sung our history and they keep on doing it. They can remember the whole history of Mali; of the most important families; of any single member; what happened to the head of the family, to the wives and cousins, and all of this by chanting with amazing talent!

Griots and the female *griottes* are very well-known figures on the artistic scene, singing in nightclubs and during summer festivals, thus commodifying their traditional role as history-tellers, which now only survives within the boundaries of the Soninké enclaves. The griots, as much as the iron-makers (see following section), are castes in their own right, meaning that their status is hereditary and that marriage, although not endogamous, is only allowed within their caste. During public celebrations, the *griottes* are exempt from cooking, a duty that is instead carried out by professional cooks or ordinary women.

Once, the residents organised a special night to create a little festive atmosphere. The canteen remained open until midnight, and food was provided throughout the day and during the celebration. People from the Soninké community also attended the venue. The griot sang his repertoire for hours, while a number of people gave him money during the performance, intervening with dance moves and engaging with the griot in the midst of applauses and cheers. Women from the community and a few cooks from the canteen also participated in the dances, creating a very joyful and entertaining moment.

Donations, or *sadaqah*, testify to the value of the recipients for the community. They can be made on various occasions and with different purposes, such as at Muslim and community celebrations and when visiting a marabout. In the village, the exchange may entail the gift of food, artefacts and fabric. As non-monetary, emotional and even ritual forms of reciprocity, compensation and obligation are crucially interconnected even in economic transactions (Shipton 2007, 2010), it is upon migration that money has become the common currency with which to express gratitude, and has acquired, in turn, social value. Even though the gift of money should be optional and according to the means of the person, to give too little, even among the residents, is shameful.

In the Sahel region, with the impoverishment of the arable lands due to the desertification process, the importance of technical equipment for irrigation supersedes that of agricultural labour. Thus, the input of revenues, sought through migration, both regional and transnational, is now estimated to be of greater value than that of goods, and thus engenders greater monetarisation in both social and family relationships, whereby affection is expressed through the distribution of material resources (Coe 2011). In the rural communities, the women whose husbands have migrated are totally dependent on their husbands' parents and family, who control them and the money that their husbands send home, further diminishing the latter.

Although tensions are not a rare occurrence at Foyer93, these are generally not due to class divisions. Caste provides stability and order in the *foyer* by traditionally embodying the material and spiritual needs of the residents, such as prayer, healing, craftsmanship, leadership and even celebration; in sum, the main elements of the Soninké society.

The Iron-Makers

The iron-makers' caste is, as such, hereditary and initiatory, its members descending from the lineage of *forgerons* (iron-makers), and is made up of two main families. The first is the Fané, of Bambara descent, the 'pure *forgerons*', while the second is the Kanté, of Malinké ancestry, also called *cadets* (the young ones) because they are descended from warriors and slaves who married into the iron-maker families at the time of Soumaworo Kanté. Warriors could demand weapons and armour from the iron-makers, but a few also joined them in their production and stayed on even after the wars (Kante 1993: 28). The *forgerons* cannot marry people from other *nyamakala*, castes – lit. 'carriers of occult power', in whose respect 'they are superior' (ibid.: 25). Men work the iron and wood and are responsible for circumcising male children, thus marking their entry into the *koma cult* or cult of the jinns, the spirits. Women are *potiers*, makers of vases, as they work the clay and are responsible for female excision. The iron-makers are considered to have a privileged relationship with the 'jinns of the earth, wind and fire' (ibid.: 15), as they work with fire, and they are conceived as the 'most educated people' for being 'the initiators to all the great domains of society' (ibid.: 25). Their knowledge, with which they are endowed by the jinns, allows them to master divination, healing and craftsmanship, and to intervene in marriage disputes.

In the middle of the court of Foyer93 is the forge, at which about ten *forgerons* work every day from dawn until dusk. Their hammering resonates in every corner of Foyer93. The forge looks like a cave, as it has the shape of a dome made of brick walls (contrary to the tailor's workshop). The floor is laid in clay, upon which big rectangular stones serve as seats, which are positioned next to the source of fire, fuelled by a power hose. All around are buckets of water, used to cool down the red-hot steel or gold. The forge stands as another compound, beyond the cafeteria, the market stands and the tailor's workshop. Nobody is allowed in besides the *forgerons*, as nobody can practise in their lieu. This rule is very firmly adhered to even in Paris, contrary to the practice of a healer, who can carry out divination without belonging to a maraboutic family.

Simaga, 30, and Sambaké, a year younger, are *forgerons* from the village of Diafouné. They used to be residents of Foyer93, which they now attend for their daily activity. They came to France by plane, as they put it, as if to say that they did not reach Europe by boat, thus distancing themselves from those who did and who, of course, had fewer means than they did. Simaga speaks impeccable French, a knowledge that dates back to his schooling in Kayes. As Gounongbé (2009) has pointed out, often the effort that is required of the migrant to settle in France has already taken place in Africa; he defines this as 'colonisation *intra muros*' (ibid.: 33). Sambaké is an iron-maker by family tradition; he works both at Foyer93 and at his workshop in Paris. He learned the job from his father by producing simple tools alongside him. He explained to me that each iron-maker has their own *jinni* (جيني) (pl. jinn) and that the jinns choose you when you have acquired enough experience and maturity. He admitted to not having one yet, but said that he knows how to work, and can produce jewellery on demand and afford to reside outside Foyer93.

The iron-makers have their own routine in the *foyer* and mingle very little with the other residents. Overall, no one interferes with their job out of respect, while a few others like Sylla, a resident from Sambaga, condemn the *forgerons* as 'bad Muslims'. Among the iron-makers are a few from the 'pure' families of *forgerons*, reputed to have divinatory and healing powers, because of their connection with the spiritual realm. According to the Islamic tradition, the jinns are the hidden doubles of humans. There are many and they are of different species. There can be Muslim jinns as much as Muslim iron-makers' jinns. The marabouts, the imams and the great village leaders also have them. Being part of the iron caste implies that your father's or grandfather's jinns is passed on to you. In other words, even among the *forgerons'* families, not every member is made part of the secret. The jinns are said to inspire the work and provide guidance. It is vital that he who has one does not betray it. The jinns appear in human form, or when invisible, manifest themselves by asking for allegiance in exchange for power. Allegiance to the jinns implies a pact of honesty and purity.

The iron-makers in Paris produce jewellery of the utmost beauty for the general public, both African and French, although the spiritual dimension of their craftsmanship is curtailed at Foyer93. Decisions continue to be made by the families back home, where only the elders among the iron-makers are consulted. Their role in the diaspora has become a lay one, since the majority of them are believed not to have a spirit guide yet. Their expertise is rather more practical than ritual and limited to what they may have learned before leaving Kayes. As Simaga explained, their domain is all to do with fire:

> If somebody gets burned or there is smoke involved, they call us. This has already happened in the canteen: there had been a great leak of smoke and one of the cooks fainted. We went over and helped resuscitate the lady. Another time, one got burned and bled from having cut herself too. She came up to us, the blood still trickling down from her hand. We pronounced a few [ritual] words and the blood stopped immediately. When we do that, everything disappears. You won't even be able to see a scar!

At Foyer93 there used to be an old iron-maker who carried out circumcisions. Unfortunately, he eventually returned to Kayes and had done so by the time of my fieldwork. His departure put a stop to my understanding of this central social and ceremonial practice and of the relationship it fosters between Foyer93 and the Soninké community outside of it. I heard from Sambaké:

> He was an old resident and he was also the only one who could do circumcisions. Young people cannot do it; it's not the technicality of it that is difficult. It's that you must have your jinn passed on to you. What the iron-maker says during circumcision is secret and it's not from the Qur'an either. During the ritual, the iron-maker cuts the skin of the male child and blood comes

out, but we can make the child recover much more quickly than if he went to the hospital. Many now go to the hospital, as they are afraid that it might not be too hygienic.

As Last has argued, the 'West African spirit realm has shrunk on contact with the West' and, if this is the trend, 'traditional healing will be limited to simply herbal knowledge for physical ailments' (2007: 7).

Family and Gender Relationships

Foyer93 is entirely dominated by a male population, so the question that confronts the anthropologist here is whether or not Malian women have migrated with their spouses; and if so, where do they live?

After Independence, and as a consequence of the droughts that struck the Sahelian regions in the 1970s, France witnessed an increase in the number of migrants from West Africa. Amendments were introduced to the 1945 ordinance of the Common Law, regulating the migrants' right to sojourn and acquire French nationality, and these de facto excluded African people. Then, the 1986 Pasqua Law restricted family reunions, which could henceforth only occur once and involve one spouse and their children. However, African families do not always correspond to the European standard of nuclear families[2] (Brunet 2010), so that with racism and discrimination also contributing, these migrants have been prevented from attaining a family life. By the 1980s, migration from Senegal, Mali, Mauritania and Zaire reached more than twenty thousand people in France. According to the 1999 census, by the 1990s migrants from other African states, such as the Congo, Ivory Coast, Madagascar and Cameroon (the first two being swept by civil war), had appeared (Barou 2002). INSEE figures for the period 1999–2004 show an increase of 45 per cent in the old migratory groups, with the number of Malians (35,978) second only to Senegalese (53,859), and with men still outnumbering their female counterparts. By 2019, migration stabilises at 9.9 per cent, against 7.4 per cent in 1975 and 5 per cent in 1946, while female migration reaches 51 per cent, against 44 per cent in 1975 and 45 per cent in 1946.[3]

Anthropological studies on migration have generally focused on the role of young people in affecting traditional norms and behaviours within and outside their milieu. My study in turns confirms and counters this trend, since it construes change as the effect of decisions taken by a specific generation of migrants that now corresponds, coincidentally, to the elders. They were the first to settle in Paris and to engender separation from the village by leaving their spouses behind. Their choice stood for the realisation that it was neither possible to return home nor to constitute a family in Paris. First, they paid the price of being the target of the 1974 law, with the closure of borders, and then of the Pasqua Law, becoming the generation that marked the passage from circular migration to the current international migrations. Many opted for family reunions, but others, as testified by the ageing population of the *foyers*, decided not to. This phenomenon is a pressing concern and certainly a new chapter in the long history of battles carried out by grassroots associations for the recognition of migrants' rights. The *foyers*, in fact, are not equipped for elderly residents, who are fragile people, often with health problems and in need of comfort and peace.

The old residents are a bitter reminder of what it would be to live without family, such that the new generation from Mali now envisage having a spouse – either French or Malian – in France, something that does not necessarily bypass polygynous families, but would certainly entail leaving Foyer93 for good. Those in their late thirties and over are likely to be married to more than one spouse and to have three or more children. Their wives and children are in Kayes. Single men are the youngest migrants at Foyer93 and, in most cases, their families have already chosen their future wives. Traditional marriage foregrounds the agreement of the families before the union is sanctioned by the marabout. Weddings can be carried out in Mali, in the presence of the marabout, the spouses' parents and the bride, even without the husband-to-be himself. There can be exceptions, like Makalou. He had been in France since he was 16 and was in his forties at the time of my fieldwork. He was always single throughout his sojourn in Paris. He acquired a certain economic viability and planned his return carefully, since he was always a *sans-papier*. Makalou is from Sadiola, the location of one of the most important gold mines in West Africa. He had good contacts in the local administration and his plan was to return permanently to Sadiola to work in the mine with dependants of his. He managed to do so once he cleared his status. Towards the end of my fieldwork, he left Paris. He knew that he would marry 'at least three or four women once there [in Sadiola]!' The preparation for the wedding(s) had been a long and eagerly awaited life project. Not only do the families of the future spouse(s) have to agree to the union, it can also only be carried out once the future husband has achieved enough financial viability to provide for his future wife (or wives) and children. The love between the spouses is by no means the only criterion leading to marriage.

The Soninké tradition upholds marital status above all. Women are encouraged to marry, since outside marriage they have no social status, apart from that of being under the father's authority. Widows are supposed to marry one of the husband's brothers (a custom known as levirate), so that their marital status and financial security remain unchanged. Divorce rarely occurs and is mostly a result of the husband's decision. Soninké women have little social power or control over decision-making. Although the question of the African family is central (Hannaford 2017), migration impacts on affection, reworking family ties and most importantly contributing to a broader process of class (Yount-André 2020) and social regeneration (Cole and Groes 2016; Feldman-Savelsberg 2016).

Fofana, a 25-year-old resident of Foyer93 from Gori, is married to two wives who both live in Kayes. When I asked whether he wished to bring one to Paris, he replied:

> Why? They are happy over there! The family looks after them; they have all they need. If one came to France, I could not afford the expense: we would have to find a place of our own. At least at the beginning, she would not be working or speak French or have anything to do. And the children? Plus, women become 'impolite' over here!

In Fofana's view, shared by other residents, France is a place where family values are corrupted, as opposed to Mali, where they are sustained through the authority of the community and the family. Most dread their women gaining greater freedom, which starts in Paris with the latter's entry into work and associations. Associations allow women to come out of their isolation and reconsider their position both within the family and in society. Thus, men (in the *foyers*) fear that their status in the family will be diminished by their wives' independence, especially when combined with the transmission of traditional values, at the centre of which are family roles. Nonetheless, younger generations favour the idea of settling in Paris, especially considering that both male and female young Soninkés occupy a weak social position in their society, which is patriarchal and based on the authority of the elderly.

M&S shared its findings with me about cases of family reunions that had been unsuccessful. In particular, there was one of a woman who had had a very tense marriage, which did not last. According to the Soninké custom, she should have returned to Kayes, but she sought the help of M&S because she wanted to stay and because her traditional marriage did not allow her to claim any rights vis-à-vis the French law. Therefore, M&S ensured that she and her children found a place in a hostel for single mothers. M&S could not disclose further details for privacy and security reasons, so I could not ascertain whether the husband went on living in Paris with other community members or if he had gone back to the *foyer*. In the latter eventuality, though, he would still fall into the category of 'single' resident, which conforms to the status of all the res-

Figure 4.1. The cooks at the canteen of Foyer93. © R. Hammadi.

idents in the *foyers*. Thus, the only presence of women at Foyer93, like in any other *foyers,* is that of the *cuisinières*, the cooks.

The cooks spend a good deal of time at Foyer93, and their relationship with the residents is friendly. One of the residents once said jokily that the cooks are their spouses. As a result of their own migratory experience, the latter are aware of the residents' problems and of the issues concerning Foyer93, which they share. If AFTAM decided to get rid of the 'communitarian canteen' in favour of a professional restaurant (as previously discussed), they would lose their jobs. They share in the residents' lives more than anyone else: not even the residents' wives, in fact, participate in the everyday lives of their husbands, who after all are abroad. Given that the vision of the wife, in Mali as much as in large parts of West Africa more widely, corresponds to the one who looks after her husband, gives him food once he is back home, chats with him about the day and so forth, then the cooks at Foyer93 are indeed, figuratively, the residents' spouses. In any case, the residents view them as some of the few who make a difference for them in Paris. In addition, they love the African food that the cooks prepare: they find it nutritionally complete and appetising. Western and African conceptualisations of bodily beauty, together with their culinary habits, vary greatly, as much as food choices between different social classes (Littlewood 1995; Popenoe 2003). For these West African residents, a good meal is one that is tasty and filling, far from the ideas of healthy and diet food in vogue in the West nowadays.

The cooks do not have to buy the food themselves: it is delivered to Foyer93 in large quantities by van and paid for through the earnings of the canteen. The residents deal with both delivery and payment, under the supervision of the *délégué*. The workers at the canteen also have their meals there, once the food is ready and before the peak hours start (12.30–2.30 p.m.), without sharing the common areas where the men sit. They use the toilets on the second floor as men do, which is quite inconvenient, yet they have no choice. Moreover, the custom-led organisation of Foyer93 enacts strict control over the residents and nobody would dare to harass the workers, since they would be caught immediately. The cooks engage very little with the residents and only occasionally greet some of them when they pass quickly through the court. Rumour has it that a few among them also work as prostitutes. Nevertheless, such gossip may simply be dictated by the residents' frustrated desire or their misconceptions about women who earn money.

Young residents may also have partners[4] who occasionally attend the *foyer*. The residents' romantic relationships develop like any other in which the partners live apart, except that they can never reciprocate hospitality. Of course, they deplore the situation, finding it disempowering, since their girlfriends can always 'tell them to go, when they are angry', or because their sexual lives have to take place in cheap hotels or friends' houses, an impediment that recalls the Foucauldian institutional control of the body. At Foyer93, this is extremely evident. The residents' lives are fractured: their families are in Kayes, or perhaps existing some time in the future; their sentimental lives are somewhere in Paris; their sexual experiences are often obtained through prostitution in and outside of Foyer93;[5] and their social and leisure activities, very limited within the *foyer*, mainly occur in cafes, bars or nightclubs.

The residents' relatives, too – aunts, sisters and cousins – pay visits on Fridays after prayer, and sometimes at the weekend, to bring presents or news about the family. At times, they also go to ask little favours, as Sylla once told me:

> My cousin came last Friday because she wanted a leather jacket: she knew I could find it cheaply in Paris. She came and we spent some time together, we had some food. She came with her little son as well; it was nice.

The visits serve the purpose of reinforcing family bonds and possibly of making the residents' lives less harsh. They do not last long since, especially at weekends, the majority of the residents are at Foyer93: between the ordinary residents and the visitors, the rooms become even more crowded than they normally are. Nephews are also brought along, much more often than nieces, as according to the rules of the extended family, the former are the residents' 'sons'. Sometimes children are left for a couple of days with their uncles at Foyer93, so that they can experience the *foyer* community and get their slice of community life. Cultural transmission, upon migration, also passes through the *foyers*.

Conflict and Conflict Resolution

As seen, the community helps its members by providing a place to stay, a meal and even financial support at the very beginning of their migratory experience, when the newly arrived migrant still needs to find his base. Nevertheless, the residents cannot guarantee help for too long, and conflict or ostracism may also take place. In this section, I intend to analyse what engenders conflict at Foyer93 and what strategies are put into place to solve it. I will develop the argument according to three issues: illness, security and age.

Salif (previously mentioned) is quite illustrative of the first scenario. He had come to France from Kayes independently, since his brother had already left Paris and returned home: he had been diagnosed with syphilis at stage three, the stage also responsible for mental illness, as M&S reported. Salif came to know of the existence of the Soninké *foyer* in Montreuil and decided to try his luck there. Unfortunately, though, he was refused access. He had nobody who could vouch for his entry. He slept outside Foyer93 for a few months until M&S intervened and found him a place on the ground floor. After a few months, he became ill and was diagnosed with the same illness as his brother. Salif never admitted suffering from mental illness, even when he was informed of his diagnosis. He thought that somebody had cast an evil eye on his family. Salif was abandoned to himself. The residents replied to his greetings, but they would otherwise ignore him. At Foyer93, a person with a disease, as long as they are not a burden and do not put anyone at risk, is simply tolerated. Salif is not the only person to bear the signs of sickness or suffering, as unfortunately, there are many like him at Foyer93. One man, who bumped into me as I entered the *foyer* one afternoon, stopped me in tears and described how miserable his life was and how much it had deteriorated. Many residents stated that their life was better before migration, in that the quality of life, if anything, was at least human: one of poverty, but not of degradation. He told me:

> I sleep in the canteen at night; we are all crammed in there, it's noisy and it's hard to get a little sleep. It stinks and it's inhuman. In my village I would at least sleep in my bed at night!

Everyone has his load to carry and tries not to make it heavier by getting involved in other people's concerns. In a way, this is survival rather than indifference. In fact, roommates have a sense of each other's well-being. They spend a lot of time together, and in a context of a total lack of privacy, so changes of mood or uncharacteristic behaviours do not pass unnoticed. There was one episode with an old resident, Diallo. He was 70 and had already retired. He had a hard time settling into his new life without going to work, thus having to spend most of his time at Foyer93. Without a job, the residents have few places to go to, especially when by doing so they increase the chances of incurring police checks. Diallo restricted his outings more and more, until he stopped going out altogether. He dressed in a work outfit and consumed only milk and bread, nutrition with clear metaphorical symbolism. He started losing a lot of weight and alienating himself from the others. His behaviour alarmed his roommates, who signalled the fact to the *délégué*, and, by word of mouth, the news spread. When M&S set up its periodic health checks, it was informed of the case. M&S started psychological therapy with him at Foyer93 and, as soon as his health had begun to improve, he continued with a psychologist at the hospital in Montreuil. M&S also supported him with the bureaucratic procedures for obtaining social support and his pension,[6] to which he was entitled.

At Foyer93, the elderly people enjoy their status as *aînés* (old people), who are traditionally those who have a voice in the so-called *arbre à palabre*, or the 'tree of discussions'. In the rural areas in Africa, men gather under the trees where, sheltered by their shadow, they discuss the problems of the village, litigations, projects and so forth. The traditional leader of the village, the sages and the old men take part in these meetings. At Foyer93, the old residents have no effective decisional power. As it has been pointed out, the new *arbre à palabre* in France is the Consultation Council. The *délégués*, who may also be the sages or village leaders, are those who deal with the issues of Foyer93. Nevertheless, solutions are not necessarily worked out at the CC meetings, which, as I showed above, can instead be the grounds for contention, as AFTAM's and the residents' views rarely overlap. There are matters such as that of the collective savings, which are regulated internally. The residents collect the money towards emergencies, to run Foyer93 and for the repatriation of the dead. This practice has existed in the *foyer(s)* since the very beginning, when migrants realised that they could not deal with crises without organisation, as resorting to loans from the bank would not be an option. The treasurer is responsible for keeping the money, which in the past was kept in his locker at Foyer93, until an armed group of criminals entered Foyer93, raided it, killed the treasurer and escaped with the money. The amount was substantial, considering that it was the monthly savings towards which about one and a half thousand people contributed with at least ten euros each. Both Djibril, the imam, and Makalou accounted for the episode, which of course is of extreme gravity for its violence and breach of internal security. As the imam told me:

> At Foyer93 there are traitors and spies. We don't know who they are and that's why [it] is safer to keep on our guard at all times. Nobody from outside Foyer93 could have possibly known about the money, its exact location and who the treasurer was. Obviously, information leaked from the inside. After that, the police raided Foyer93 one night: they banged with their truncheons at every single door and made a lot of noise. They scared everyone. I think that they wanted to warn us and show that we are under control!

Following this brutal episode, the residents were shattered and paralysed. They did not respond immediately, especially because the lack of trust and fear hindered the possibility of discussing the issue further. They understood that keeping the money physically at Foyer93 was too dangerous and no longer viable. The problem was brought to the attention of the president of the *délégués*, the *sages*, the imam and other ranking people such as the marabout. At Foyer93, like in the village, decisions are taken on the basis of a collective discussion. The proponents and decision-makers are not the older residents per se, but the representatives of the different villages and their delegates sitting in the Consultation and Residents Councils. As for the savings, they decided that the money should be placed thenceforth in a bank account, so they opened one into which anyone can now put his share. Since then, other saving accounts have been opened for different purposes. One of these, for example, is used for the mosque in the *foyer* and for the construction of a new mosque in Mali. This is, of course, under the imam's responsibility: he is the only person who has access to the account and who can collect the money. The savings concerning Foyer93 are under the *délégués*' control, and those regarding the migrants' associations and co-ops under that of their leaders. The latter are often also the founders, or might happen to be the traditional leaders of their villages, but not invariably.

In Kayes, a great deal of the total revenue is provided by the migrants' remittances. The migrant retains his role in the family by coordinating the family interest through those who have not migrated themselves (his father, brothers or eldest son). When there are expenses required or disagreements, he is always consulted, through the numerous conversations that take place over the phone. The residents' translocality is unquestionable. This is not only true for the younger migrants, but also for the elderly ones, whose presence is increasing in the *foyers* of Paris. Traditionally, the elders should be the heads of their *ka* and should supervise the work of the younger members. It is important to appreciate that their role is fundamental in family relationships, as they make decisions regarding the education of the children, the managing of family finances and properties, the choice of future partners for their sons and daughters, and so forth. In the diaspora, senior migrants send their remittances home as any other male member of the family does, but all the while, their say in the *foyer* is of little value, and the intergenerational gap widens, spurring conflict.

At Foyer93, the old people suffer the most in the transition from the old migratory pattern to the current one. When they migrated, they were the first to initiate co-development projects, which saw the importance of migrants' input into the local economy. Historical changes take place over different generations, and so it has been for Kayes. The 'old men of Foyer93' were still subjected to the customary rule of their own elders who had not migrated. As Lavigne Delville (1991) showed, migrants' associations in Mali attempted to bring about innovation while maintaining customary relationships: the elders supervised the large-scale irrigation system that had been set up by the young, that is, the migrants. Nevertheless, given the increasing poverty of the region of Kayes and the never-ceasing migratory flows, the model within which these relationships play out has radically changed. Contemporary international circulations feature a generation of people, both young and not so young, migrating *en masse*. Upon migration, they create their own hierarchies of authority. At Foyer93, those who opened the way are those who are now left out. This is palpable in the gossip and jealousies that are widespread at Foyer93. Barka, an old resident from the village of Sambaga, once said, dismissing the delegates' work: 'They are the delegates of what? They represent nobody here, apart from the women.'

Considering the role of women within the Soninké community, Barka was stating his derogatory view of the delegates as men of no responsibility – if men at all! Elders like Barka sit together in the court, chat away during the day, but have little contact with the other residents. They are indeed a minority within the minority. Although they have engendered and been the prelude to the new phase of international migrations, these have eventually disempowered them. Those who have not returned home permanently or moved out of Foyer93 pay the price of a changing society, one that builds wealth on the global market through projects and dynamism. The old residents, aged 60 and over, manage to keep their status marginally, either among their family members or among their age group. In the current scenario, both the roles of the elders and of the existing hierarchies are undergoing a reconfiguration. Tradition, far from being abandoned, is being moulded after the rules of the diaspora, a ferocious world increasingly characterised by uncertainty and survival.

Notes

1. Greetings of this kind would take place in both French and Soninké. This is my rendition in English.
2. There are certainly West Africans who live in nuclear families in France and Europe, but among migrants from the rural areas of Kayes, they were surely rare in the 1980s.
3. See https://www.insee.fr/fr/statistiques/3633212 (accessed 20 November 2020).
4. Homosexuality is strongly disavowed both religiously and socially in this context (due to both Muslim and traditional mores), so I could never address this topic in order to learn more.
5. My position as a female researcher made it impossible to shed more light on issues related to sexuality and prostitution, which were unequivocally engaged in by residents of the *foyers*.
6. Migrants who are entitled to a pension scheme must spend a period of at least three months per year in France, which makes it impossible for them to leave France for good.

5

Islam at Foyer93 and in the Île-de-France

The Practice of Islam in the *Foyers*

The practice of Islam among the Soninké migrants has seen different phases, which correspond to the chronology of their accommodation process (Timera 1996).[1] During the 1960s, Islam was not frequently practised in the *foyers*. Much like in the Islamic conception of *dar al-harb* (دار الحرب), the land where Islam is absent, as opposed to *dar al-Islam* (دار الاسلام), the land of Islam, this generation of migrants thought of their stay in France as temporary and did not aim to put down roots. In the 1970s and 1980s, mobility to France became more and more prevalent, such that the community was confronted by the necessity of reformulating Islam transculturally, that is, of finding ways to practise it abroad and to justify worship in the *kafir* (كافر) lands. The Soninkés started to open their own *daawas* (الدعوة) Sufi orders, inspired in their most rigorist reform movement by the Wahabyya. Their faithful were called *sunna-gummu*, as they advocated a return to the 'purest' tradition of the Sunna. In the end, the movement could not create an alternative to the essentially political and social organisation of the Soninké community in France (ibid.: 252).

The first Soninké *daawas* in France, which gathered a host of worshippers, was founded by Mamadou Diana, from the village of Soninkara, Mali. He studied the Qur'an in France, and only after his return from Morocco in 1974 did he start preaching at his *daawa* among his compatriots, spreading his message around the Soninké *foyers* in Paris,

Le Havre and Lille. Timera suggests that the growth and success of the *daawa* was intended to provide the Soninkés of France with a motivation to practise Islam; back in the village such a role was fulfilled by the family and the *moodi*, marabout, both absent after migration. Qur'an and Arabic classes started taking place in the *foyers*, enhancing the importance of literate individuals and intellectuals, such as the imams, over the marabouts. Among the Soninkés in France, the Islamic awakening meant a move away from the lineage authority in favour of the clerics, in contrast to the latter's secondary role back in the village. Mamadou Diana was later assassinated, his death apparently linked to his project of building a mosque. The role of the *daawa* lost vigour, so much so that Islam among the Soninkés is now more a matter of personal devotion than a phenomenon organised around a *daawa* (ibid.: 175–78).

Diop and Michalak inform us that the first mosque in a 'black African residence appeared in 1967 at the ground floor of foyer *La Commanderie*', in the nineteenth borough of Paris. 'In 1977, a second foyer' opened its doors to a mosque, and 'now almost all of them have prayer rooms, which are subsidized by all residents of the foyer, whether Muslim or not. The UNAFO, the principal organization of black African *foyers*, has 126 *foyers* in the Île-de-France region of which 119 have prayer rooms' (1996: 82).

The Imam at Foyer93

At Foyer93, Friday prayers take place in the court, since the prayer room is very small. The imam is Djibril. He is a man in his sixties, from the village of Gory, Mali. He came to France in the 1970s, when the increased Soninké and, more broadly, African migration to France enjoyed fewer restrictions and more adequate job opportunities. He now has four wives and twelve children who live in the village. As he states, any journey to Gory is an occasion to increase the family: during my fieldwork in Paris, he went back once for the birth of his baby girl. He has retired, but according to the law, he has to reside for at least three months in France in order to obtain his pension; Djibril thus returns to Africa at least once a year. The Centre Allocations Familiales (Family Allowance Centre, CAF) carries out regular checks on the actual presence of retired migrants in France by checking the stamps on their passports. The same procedure is not applied to retired French citizens.

At Foyer93, Djibril lives on the second floor with his family members: two brothers, three cousins and a nephew. His status grants him a privileged position, and thus the chance to live with his family in a quieter area of the *foyer*, as the rooms on the lower floors are noisier than those in the upper ones. Nonetheless, given the increasing number of people in the *foyers*, more and more frequently people pour into his room at night, begging for some space to crash on. Djibril is a friend of Farid, the owner of the local laundry, a man of Algerian origin in his forties and also a Muslim. They meet to chat about their lives, their home countries and Islam. Often Djibril spends hours, even after dark, at the laundry. He and Farid keep each other company, since they have consolidated a good friendship. Over time, I got to know Farid better, and he told me about Djibril's uncomfortable life at Foyer93. Due to either decency or shame, Djibril would rarely talk about it with me.

Following his retirement, Djibril spends a lot of time at Foyer93. He can relax in the afternoons, taking advantage of having the room to himself when his family members have gone to work or are simply out. In the mornings, people take turns to clean the floor and even to iron his garments, duties that his wives would otherwise carry out back home. His landline phone rings constantly as people ask for his services, such as carrying out ceremonies and funerals according to the Muslim ritual. He learned the Qur'an at a *madrasa* (المدرسة القرآنية), a Qur'anic school in the village; he speaks fair French and, most of all, he reads Arabic, which is quite unheard of among the residents. Arabic is not only the sacred language of the Qur'an, it is the language of erudite people throughout the Muslim world.

Djibril is also in charge of the savings for the mosque. Donations are made especially during *zakāt* (الزكاة), the annual tithe and one of the five pillars of Islam, which sanctions the obligation to help people in need and the poor generally. The residents donate their money to him, who, once he has collected a considerable amount, places it into the dedicated account. The imam is the only one who has the code for the account and who can withdraw the money, which is sometimes used as an extra source of revenue when the village savings are insufficient. There are as many savings accounts as the villages represented at Foyer93.

Djibril has little contact with the other residents in the courtyard, although he receives many visits in his room, such as from the delegates. They inform him about the proceedings of the Residents Committee and of the problems at Foyer93, which are not few and far between. The way that the clerical and lay management of Foyer93 intertwine can be witnessed during these briefings. While the delegates stand for the practical aspects of Foyer93 and its external relations, the imam acts as the main Muslim representative in the *foyer*. In the face of unsolved disputes among the residents, after the roommates and the delegates have intervened, the imam is the one who is called upon. Islam, for many of them, is not a matter of choice, but something within which they have grown up, and a 'good' Muslim, beyond respecting the precepts of Islam, is somebody who is 'proper', as they put it. On the contrary, a 'bad' Muslim would be somebody who brings a degree of pollution or disorder, whether symbolic or physical, quite resonant with Mary Douglas's (2002) conceptualisation of both purity and danger. There is a sense of legitimate versus illegitimate behaviour, according to which one knows immediately if a resident follows what is perceived to be good practice. Spending too much time at the cafeteria or outside the *foyer* at night and not praying during the day can be indications of one's misbehaviour. To incur the residents' negative opinion bears consequences and nobody wishes to be the object of these judgements, as they will eventually reflect on one's family's reputation too. The village community expands and overlaps with the diasporic community in Paris, so that there is too much at stake for them not to adhere, if not formally, to the rules of Foyer93. Foyer93 is the new 'village' for the residents, who now turn to the diasporic community of Paris for their daily needs and companionship, while abiding by both its rules and hierarchy, and the Parisian way of life.

At Foyer93, Islam translates into an organisational system that can mobilise and sanction the residents' behaviour more strongly than the authority of a delegate can. When the residents say that the delegates deal with everything in the *foyers*, they put two concepts forward. The first is that the delegates are the main people with whom the French authorities deal with regard to the management of the *foyer*, while the second foregrounds that what goes on internally is regulated by community or tradition (or both), and that it is for nobody else to interfere with. Arguably, it is not the practice of Islam that intensifies upon migration, but rather the community bond that is created through it. The residents perform the ablutions, carry out the ritual prayer and mingle together afterwards. The imam's and the elders' moral reproach of those who spend a lot of time in the cafeteria also aims at targeting the new (generally younger) residents and alienating them. The residents adopt strategies of inclusion and exclusion to integrate or marginalise types of residents, whom they perceive as a threat. Newcomers are but one example of danger or alterity, which is predicated and tested through the vocabulary of Islam.

The Marabout

In the Maghreb and sub-Saharan countries, the term marabout or *cheick* is used to identify the spiritual leader, often the head of a *zawiya* (الزاوية) – a sacred pilgrimage centre – or the initiator of a Sufi order, who is bound to perpetuate his teaching as a *muqaddam* (مُقَدَّم). The marabout – a French (and English) adaptation of the Arabic term *murabit* (المرابط) – their followers and the phenomenon of Sufi Islam, with its orders, the *tariqa*, are common knowledge in France. The marabout is the unique master of his *talibés* (طالبان), or followers, who resort to his spiritual knowledge to be guided in both their ordinary and devout lives. Marabouts are part of a caste system that is passed on through generations, in which the clerics enjoy the highest status, followed by the iron-makers and the griots. The West African cultural landscape is also dotted with figures such as the traditional healers, who are reputed to be in connection with the supernatural realm thanks to their *baraka* (البركة), God-given gift, which allows them to deal with the jinns. The latter are part of a religioscape within which health and well-being are understood and managed, as at its core is the notion that the jinns control illnesses (Last 2007). Healers are thought to disclose the cause of illnesses and tackle their effects in nature (Sow 1980), while the marabout is conceived of as linking the immediate reality of suffering to Allah (الله), to Whom he addresses his prayers. In fact, different forms of intelligence outline an Islamic cosmogony whose signs, *ayat* (آيات), inform humankind of its divine nature. This realisation, *tahaqouq* (التحقّق), is the primal step into Islam, which is *submission* to this truth, and thus the first obligation of a Muslim (Turner 1996).

According to my respondents, the ontological complexity of *baraka* adds to the confusion for Europeans in identifying a marabout as opposed to a healer or one who practises magic, *sahar* (سحر), all of whom are equally downgraded to charlatans. *Barkat* (بركات) is only one term among several, which specifically refers to a particular form of saintly power that is not only for healing and exorcism.

Islam in Mali was introduced by Cheick Ahmed Hamallah (1883–1943), the founder of the eponymous Sufi brotherhood, the Hammalliyya, a schismatic branch of the principal Tijaniyya order that split over the controversy of the so-called 'eleven grains' (Traoré 1983).[2] When I enquired about the figure of Cheick Hamallah at Foyer93, my respondents admitted that there were still a few affiliates in the region of Kayes. However, the Hammalliyya has developed into a marginal phenomenon in Mali, while the marabout has lost his role as spiritual guide, becoming instead the dispenser of Qur'anic teaching. At Foyer93, this function is carried out by the imam, who has thus come to the forefront as the Soninkés' Muslim representative in the diaspora.

In Soninké society, the *modinu*, marabout, belonged to the lowest rank of freemen, the *hooro*, in a ruler's entourage, after princes, advisors and warriors. As noted by Jamous (1981), they were set apart from the rivalries of the segmentary society, which was ravaged by the fighting of different groups for power over the land, and lived in their own compounds. The marabout marked the moment of ceasefire, in which the fighting groups settled their blood debts of vengeance, before internal wars were triggered again by more killings and raids.

Like many others throughout Paris, the marabout whom I could meet at Foyer93, Ahmed, practises divination rituals and attends to people from the most disparate backgrounds, beyond the residents themselves. He is from Diafouné and is in his late fifties. He declared that he had his own method, which he described as a path. In his words:

> I can find answers by following my own path. It's like a route, which is not for everybody to know. All I have is my way and this prayer bead. You see? I don't need anything else.

Ahmed is renowned for his ability both to understand his clients' situations and to find a solution accordingly. His clients are expected to carry out a *sadaqah*, or donation, and when they are Muslim, they are also required to pray the *Al-Fatiha* (صَلَاة الضحى), the first sura of the Qur'an, and an extra *duha* (دَعَ), prayers of praise to God. One day, an Ivorian woman in her forties was outside the imam's room, carrying two pints of milk. The door was sealed off with Sellotape, since the room had been sprayed with pesticides. I had a meeting with the imam myself, so there we were, before one another. The woman said that she would have preferred to make her donation to the imam himself, as *sadaqah* can be offered to anyone. Thus, the first resident who approached us was given the two pints of milk. I then escorted the woman out and asked her what she had found with the marabout's help; in short, why she visited him. She responded:

> That marabout is very good. He can 'see' many things. He has helped me a lot; he has given me advice on many things. But you, young lady [referring to me], be careful! Don't hang about too much in here [Foyer93], or you'll end up married to one of them before you know [laughter]!

Kuczynski (2002, 2004) has extensively studied French religious pluralism. In particular, her case study (Kuczynski 1988) shows how often the Western clientele exoticises traditional healing because of, or together with, the 'otherness' of its practitioners, giving it the label 'magic'. In African milieus, attending a marabout is nothing exceptional, but rather part of a behaviour that is embedded in the community. Generally, the marabout is somebody of one's own entourage, if not ethnic group and religious affiliation. The residents of Foyer93 view the marabout as a savant, whose experience and spirituality enable him to see the jinns. He is considered a pure man, who can only do 'good things' for the people, but certainly not change the course of their lives. This would imply 'black magic'. Sorcerers' witchcraft can probably be summed up by the work of Evans-Pritchard (1937), in that it implies vengeance and the intention to harm somebody. The phenomenon is not only forbidden in Islam, it is also not condoned by the community, Soninké and Muslim, by and large. Hence their definition of charlatans: those who claim to be able to solve all problems, or who have no knowledge to back up their practice, which they nevertheless fake for the 'Europeans', who are thought to be gullible.

Sambaké, one of the residents of Foyer93, visits the marabout to ask advice and guidance in moments of distress and crisis. To thank the marabout, he pays him. Among the residents, the exchange of money is not a way of obtaining the marabout's best intervention, as is argued to be the case among the French audience, but a matter of expressing gratitude and respect. Verses of the Qur'an are used during consultation and repeated over the client, because 'the Qur'an itself is healing', as the sacred text itself states (17:82 and 41:44). The marabout may also produce protective amulets with words from the Qur'an written on them and ask his client to undertake an action that might be propitiatory to a good outcome, such as a *sadaqah*.

The residents admit that trustworthy marabouts do not migrate, so those who have left their country young might not have learned enough to acquire the 'secret' from their forefathers. The marabouts' personal history ensures their credibility and therefore their reputation within the community, both back home and in the diaspora. Renowned marabouts should be old enough to have practised divination rituals for a while, or to have combined this with the characteristic apprenticeship they may have inherited from the family or through journeys in West Africa, which they carry out to satisfy their spiritual quest. Practising marabouts mediate between this world and the beyond, in a fusion of the worlds akin to that described by Stoller (1989, 1995), where the metaphysical reality that they summon is the pantheon of the spirits, doubles of the people to whom they manifest. For the residents, the relationship with the invisible world is one of dialogue and not of possession. The 'tricks' that the jinns may play on people – because the latter have deceived them, walked on their territory or stepped inadvertently on them – may cause diseases that are construed as an attack. Episodes of this sort require healing that not all marabouts are able to perform (see Chapter 7).

Islam in the Île-de-France Region: The Mouridiyya

The Mouridiyya is a Sufi branch of Islam, founded in Senegal by Cheick Amadou Bamba M'Backé (henceforth Bamba) (1855–1927), which counts an increasing number of followers the world over, both among Muslims and new converts. The sacred town of Touba, Senegal, founded by Bamba in 1887, is the Mourides' stronghold as much as an organisational centre for migration, first to Dakar and then to Europe (Diouf 2000). Touba has become the second town in Senegal with 1,500,000 inhabitants, attracting millions of people for the *magal*, pilgrimage celebrating Bamba 's departure to exile. The mosque of Touba, where Bamba is interred, used to be the greatest and most prestigious one of West Africa up until 2019, when the Mouride mosque Massalikoul Djinane was erected in Dakar.[3] In fact, although Senegalese migration is now facing a new phase, in which students and intellectuals from the urban centres appear to migrate in great numbers, migration from the rural interior, such as the region of Touba, continues to be crucial, and the role of the brotherhood is in providing a network and support for its faithful before and upon migration (Ebin 1992).

Paul Marty's (1917) and Coppolani's (1897) studies marked the beginning of French colonial works on Islam in Africa, which are now criticised as proposing rather ethnocentric and superficial understandings of Islam. As Glover (2007) put it, the history of Mouridism is a history of 'intersections' and its modernity rests in its appropriation of global and local historical forces alike. At the time of the French colonial conquest, the transatlantic slave trade had ended, yet its echoes reverberated in the interior of West Africa, where the aristocracy and the jihadist Muslim leaders alike fought for their visions of the world. Bamba opposed both structures of power.

Characteristic of the Mouride brotherhood is the relationship between marabout and *talibés*, that is, between master and faithful. Cruise O'Brien (1988) has insisted on the charismatic role of the Mouride marabout towards his following based on his closeness to God, which is conceived of as granting him the divine gift of *baraka* as a *wali* (ولي), saintly man. Copans's (1980) deeply Marxist reflection on Mouridism has portrayed this relationship as one of dependence and exploitation, in a classic logic of historical materialism. This author showed that the Mouride brotherhood provided a transient structure to pre-capitalist Senegal since, it is argued, the capitalist market could not have been imported without a system such as that provided by the Mouridiyya. The passage took place in three phases: firstly, with the dissolution of the Wolof political system; secondly, with the 'French political-military conquest'; and thirdly, through the development of the peanut cash crop (ibid.:77). The foundation of the Mouridiyya coincided, in fact, with the 'colonisation' of new lands (Robinson and Triaud 1997; Coulon 1981), through a migratory trend that encompassed the old Wolof regions of Cayor and Baol towards the Jolof region (Copans 1980:79). According to Robinson (2000a), the French consolidation and policy towards the Mourides was marked by an initial phase of suspicion, during which Bamba was exiled three times (1895–1912), and a second phase of accommodation and control (1912–27). 'To put it in Gramscian terms, the French sought to create a hegemony to parallel their domination' ibid.: 77). Furthermore, the colonial administration availed itself of the cooperation of Mauritanian Muslims, often members of the Qadriyya Sufi order, believing in the superiority of the *'bidan* people over the blacks' (Traoré 1983: 87).

Gilsenan (1973) opened up an understanding of the Sufi orders as a dynamic, flourishing occurrence internal to Islam, a response to the needs of the masses and the historical changes of society against the ossification of the intellectual elite of the *ulema* (العلماء). Nonetheless, Sufism, as the mystical tradition of Islam or *tasawwuf* (التصوف), cannot unequivocally be situated in the opposition between high and low Islam or popular and doctrinal spheres (Abun-Nasr 2007). Sufism is a globalising phenomenon, which entails doctrinal and leadership controversies within the *ummah* (أمة) that have not declined over time. In Paris, the Mourides face now, as much as in the past, the Wahabis' dissent, as the latter view Sufism as idolatry; internal rivalries; and the overall suspicion of Islam by the non-Muslim French population.

There are two Mouride centres in the Île-de-France region, also called *maisons* in French or Kerr Serin[4] Touba in Wolof, meaning 'the house of the master of Touba', that is, Bamba. The one in which I carried out my fieldwork was founded in 2002 in Taverny, under the auspices of the then Khalif Serin Saliou M'Backé; the other is in Aulnay. The Aulnay Centre is regulated by the French law of 1901 by which any group has (the right) to register as an association and thus become a public entity in negotiation with the state. The Mouride Centre of Taverny has since become a fully fledged Islamic Centre, falling under the 1905 French law that marks the separation of the church from the state after the French principle of *laïcité,* secularism.[5]

The Centre stages, as it were, the Cliffordian concept of *travelling cultures* (Clifford 1992), its faithful having been able to settle down and practise their religion around the world, from Japan to the USA. Similarly, Riccio (2001, 2003) argues for a *distinctive culture of migration* capable of establishing transnational *linkages* – networks that are much more fluid than a unitary phenomenon – between the diaspora and Senegal.

It has also been pointed out that the Mourides' success lies in their Sufi work ethic (Piga 2002; Schmidt di Friedberg 1994; Carter 1997; Ebin 1996), which emphasises the training, discipline and solidarity that have guaranteed the Mouride diaspora its dynamism and intra-aid support (Bava 2004, 2010).

In the next chapter, I will analyse how the order has become one of the best expressions of Francophone Islam, leading the way to the recognition of other Muslims, be they French or Francophone, such as the Soninkés.

Notes

1. The first three sections of this chapter have been used in my forthcoming article 'France and Islam: A Contested Relationship', which will be published in the journal *Insaniyat* إنسانيات, *Algerian Journal of Anthropology and Social Sciences* in a special issue entitled 'Religion et Religiosité en Méditerranée'; see https://journals.openedition.org/insaniyat/ (accessed 18 March 2022).
2. The Hammallists claimed that the recitation of the Tijan formula *Jawaharatu-l-Kamali* (جوهرة الكمال), 'The Jewel of Perfection', should appear eleven times in the *wazifa* (وزفة), praising prayer, as posited in the main Tijan book, *Jawahir al-Ma'ani* (جواهر المعاني), 'The Jewels of Meaning', rather than twelve, as several branches of the Tijaniyya order, aligned with the French, argued. The Hammallist's prayer was also composed of two rather than four *rakas* (راكاس), prostrations, indicative of a prayer carried out quickly because of the presence of danger. During the French colonial occupation, the so called 'short prayer' symbolised the Muslim revolt against the persecuting French.
3. See: https://www.lemonde.fr/afrique/article/2019/09/27/a-dakar-l-inauguration-d-une-immense-mosquee-consacre-l-influence-des-mourides_6013343_3212.html (accessed 23 April 2022).
4. *Serin* is an honorific title meaning 'spiritual guide' in Wolof.
5. The 1905 law implies both the free exercise of religion and the non-involvement of the state in the provision of stipends to clerics or subsidies necessary to the running of religious institutions. In 2005, the centenary of the law was marked by controversies over the possibility of its abolition, raised by both the European Union, which saw it as a French oddity, and by the Sarkozian government arguing that the law only favoured Catholicism over Islam and Judaism. However, the World Humanist Congress, held at the UNESCO headquarters and at the Sorbonne University in Paris on 5–7 July 2005, defended the law as a prerequisite for a free and democratic society; https://humanists.international/policy/the-paris-declaration-2005/ (accessed 15 November 2021).

6

Francophone Islam and the Institutionalisation of the Muslim Faith

The Mouride Islamic Centre of Taverny

Within the Mouride brotherhood, as much as within the Muslim community worldwide, the question of leadership is central. So far, it has been passed on to Cheick Amadou Bamba M'Backé's direct heirs, that is, his sons of the M'Backé lineage. During the time of my fieldwork, Khalif[1] Serin Saliou was the last son of the M'Backé family, with his younger brother Serin Mourtada, the so-called 'touring marabout', strengthening the links of the community abroad. With the deaths of both Serin Saliou M'Backé (1915–2007) and Serin Mourtada M'Backé (1925–2004), Bamba's saintly descent has come to an end. In this context has arisen the Hizbut Tarqiyyah (حزب الطرقية),[2] a movement within the Mouridiyya that suggests an alternative form of leadership, one that would further the founder's message and wisdom, rather than his *silsila baraka* (سلسلة بركة), sacred lineage.

The Mourides affiliated to the Hizbut Tarqiyyah (henceforth HT) explain the movement as one that grew in the spirit of the new spiritual wave, headed in Senegal by the above-mentioned khalif, that resulted in the creation of the Union Culturelle Musulmane in 1953 by students educated in Arabic language and Studies. HT was founded in 1975 at Cheick Anta Diop University, Dakar, as the first *dahira* (الظاهرة), or Sufi urban circle, of Mouride intellectuals. They initiated a trend of reinterpretation of Bamba's opus, one that gave value to the founder's teaching

beyond its populist underpinning, which was overall limited to the pas-
sionate recounting of Bamba's ordeal during exile at the hands of the
French colonists and his eventual quasi-miraculous survival and consolidation of the Mouridiyya, which at that point had obtained an over-
whelming number of adepts. HT reached Europe in the early 1970s,
when the first Mouride students migrated from Dakar to become active
members in the universities of France and particularly of Paris. These
students set up 'Bamba Cultural Weeks', and particularly memorable
were those of 1979 at UNESCO in Paris, echoing those taking place at
Cheick Anta Diop University in Dakar, at a time when the Muslim world
generally reflected, or reacted to, the Islamic revival of the Iranian Rev-
olution. Scholars like Sëriñ Shâm Mbaye and Sëriñ Moustapha Lô also
contributed to the mission of promoting Mouridism through academic
study by organising cultural events and producing magazines such as
Ndigël. Cruise O'Brien (2003) reminds us that the 1970s were also the
time in which the drought was at its height throughout the Sahel, and
Abdou Lahatte M'Backé, third khalif of the brotherhood (1968–89),
'prompted the government publicly of its need to come to terms with the
Mouride brotherhood, for which he was the spokesman and leader'
(ibid.: 36). In 1992, Khalif Serin Saliou formalised the organisation under
the current name, opening its headquarters in the Mouride holy city of
Touba. Clearly, HT had entered a new phase, whereby it was being endorsed by the Mouride hierarchy and receiving its financial assistance,
and the future Mouride leaders would be chosen from HT cadres. HT has
now established itself throughout the world, including France.

The Mouride Islamic Centre of Taverny (henceforth MICT) is fi-
nanced by the French Council of Muslim Faith, which has the right to
its use, and by the *talibés'* self-taxation or *sas* (ساس). Khalif Serin Saliou
himself agreed to buy the space for the Centre after a delegation of Mourides from France petitioned for it. The formal signature and purchase
were carried out in the presence of the MICT's president, a Hizbut Tarqiyyah delegation from Senegal and the mayor of Taverny, who, after the
president's words, was eager to open a process of dialogue and peaceful
relations with the Muslim community.

As part of HT's project and networks, the MICT's educational goal is
paramount, attracting both researchers, who contribute to increasing
the intellectual capital of the Centre, and children, who attend the MICT
during school holidays to learn the Qur'an and Bamba's *qasidas* (قصيده)[3] or
poems. The MICT exhibits a traditional outlook, whereby the faithful
gather to pray, sing the *dhikr* (الذكر), collect the money to organise events
and generally celebrate Mouride and Muslim events alike, such as Bamba's commemorations and the *eïds.* However, alongside the religious

practice is an ongoing research endeavour in the study of Islam and of Bamba's writings and life in the face of the French colonial conquest. In this sense, the MICT conceives of itself as a reformist branch of Islam in the pursuit of the Prophet's original message, achieved through the lesson of Bamba, as much the Khadim Rassoul (خادم رسول), Servant of the Prophet, as the *mujaddid* (مجدد), the Renovator, and the *qutb* (قطب), Messenger of his time and leading saintly figure of all the centuries. The MICT hosts seminars in the fashion of academic workshops, and implements cultural projects such as the construction of the library, in the true spirit of an Islamic centre. Cheick Anta Babou, a member of Bamba's M'Backé family himself, is an exemplar of this intellectual trend within the centre. Babou is Associate Professor of African History and the History of Islam in Africa in the History Department of the University of Pennsylvania, Philadelphia. His research focuses on mystical Islam in West Africa and on the new African diaspora. He has lectured internationally and written extensively on the Mouride brotherhood (Babou 2003, 2007), and has become an important figure in the study of Sufi Islam. Therefore, the MICT is keen to divulge his and other work that exhibits a difference in the study of both the Mouride branch and the colonial presence in Africa – work that reconciles with its own understanding of these topics.

Organisation and Work:
The CREDI Khadim Rassoul and the Music Academy

The CREDI[4] Khadim Rassoul is a fundamental unit at the MICT and probably its highest accomplishment, after the mosque, representing the *ummah*, insofar as the prayer room is the symbol of Islam and its community of faith, and the *daara* (دارا), Sufi educational circle, whose mission is to impart *tarbiya* (طربية), or Islamic and spiritual learning, to children. As the president, who runs them, explained, the *daaras* are a long-standing institution within the Mouriddya. The children, both male and female, attend classes during public holidays and school vacations. Pedagogical tools have been improved to provide the young *talibés* with accessible alphabetisation, entailing the learning and reading of both the Qur'an and *qasidas*, together with workshops on *kourel* (كوريل), a particular way of chanting the *dhikr*, the Sufi remembrance of God. The Dahira Rawdu Rayahina (الظاهرة الروضه رياحينا) (Dahira Garden of Lights), led by the president's wife, is a women's Sufi urban circle. Its members attend the MICT to learn the Qur'an and the Islamic Sciences fortnightly.

Figure 6.1. Journée Qasidas at the Islamic Centre of Taverny.
© Islamic Centre of Taverny, France.

CREDI is equipped with a library as part of the fundamental facilities necessary for the dissemination of the *tariqa*'s teaching. It stores documents and books on Islam and Sufism, including copies of the Qur'an; the Prophet's tradition, that is, the Hadith and the Sunna; Muslim jurisprudence, *fiqh* (الفقة); the exegesis and commentaries of the Qur'an, *tafsir* (التفسير); the history of religions and of the hagiography of the saints of Islam; Bamba's *qasidas*; and miscellaneous works such as encyclopaedias and books of general interest in the social sciences. The library also holds an audio-visual archive, where the proceedings of Mouride conferences and events in France are stored, as well as cassettes popularising themes such as the pillars of Islam and the HT network. The book supply is guaranteed both by the MICT's purchases and by donations, and the cataloguing and digitisation of the material is underway. Finally, a media centre is also under construction, with internet access available to all, and a radio station is being set up.

Furthermore, following the Sufi tradition of the *dhikr*, the MICT has put in place a music academy of a kind, where three different *kourels* are performed. Its aim is to educate people in the techniques of vocal expression that the declamation of religious chants requires.

One of these is *adhan* (أَذَان), the call to prayer by the muezzin – a particularly important moment and a difficult performance too, due to the high-pitched tones and modulation of the sounds, also emphasised in the *kourels*, which in fact serve as a vessel for trance. A board of directors teaches the *talibés* the way to perform these and chooses the melodies in accordance with pedagogic requirements. It is important that the students perform under the direction of a guide, since the state of trance has to be sought methodically in order to avoid the haphazard loss of control into which the *talibés* might lapse. The philosophy of the music centre is that of maintaining the tradition of the *kourels* as it has been passed on for generations. Nonetheless, 'new ways of chanting are also tested in accordance with the tradition of the ancestors, *jangu makk* in Wolof', as the leading teacher explained to me. Thus, musical tradition and innovation go hand in hand at the centre.

The MICT is now a pioneering centre in France thanks to the quality of its projects and initiatives, which have even superseded those of HT in Senegal – which lags behind and relies on minor websites for the diffusion of its message – thus revealing possibilities for Islam and in particular for the Mouridiyya in Europe that are quite unique. Among several Muslim denominations, the *tariqa* has in fact become an important feature of (so-called) French Islam and of its institutionalisation, as I will show in the following sections.

The National Federation of Mourides of France

Due to France's long-term relationship with Islam, dating back to the colonial period – notwithstanding the first Muslim presence at Narbonne in the eighth century and the Muslim migrations to medieval Gaul, later France (Ahmed 2018) – Muslim associations have consolidated greater institutional weight here than in other European countries. Mouride migrants represent a relatively recent phenomenon, all the while following the old channels of West African migration to France, such as Marseille, Paris and Lyon. It is not a coincidence that the founding of the first HT took place in Paris, and that the centre for the collection of money from the different Mouride *dahiras* throughout Europe is also Paris.

The Muslim federations reflect several branches of Islam, often coinciding with the members' ethnicity or nationalities (Diop 2000),[5] but not exclusively, as the federations themselves are evolving and thus attract people from various milieus. Conversions certainly play an important role. The federations represent a milestone in the institutionalisation of the Muslim communities in France and therefore of their integration into the French social fabric, of which Islam is part and parcel. As previously mentioned, with the constitution of the French Council of Muslim Faith in 2003, the French government aimed at creating a platform of negotiation with the Muslim communities.

In 2004, with the aim of establishing a National Federation of Mourides of France (NFMF), the main Mouride institutions in France, with the help of Sëriñ Chérif M'Backé, organised national meetings in major cities such as Paris, Lyon and Toulouse. The decision to constitute strong regional federations as building blocks of the future FNMF was taken. This is how the Federations of the East, the North, the Centre and the West were born. The Southern Federation, the *Maison* of Aulnay-Sous-Bois and that of Taverny pre-existed those federations.[6] At the time, the main difficulty was the generational gap – *magg-ñi ak ndawñi* in Wolof – among the founders and their differences in socio-professional terms. In 2008, the problem was finally overcome with the renewal of the Mouride order by Khalif Sëriñ Muhammadu Lamine Bara and the deployment of emissaries to serve as mediators. That same year, all of the Mouride executives gathered at the very first meeting of the newly formed NFMF, where the foundations were laid and a national committee was drawn up among the signatories and promoters. Its first priority was the creation of Islamic Centres for the exercise of the faith and for the education of the new generations of Muslims of France. The empowerment of the *daaras,* the headquarters of Qur'anic and Muslim education, thus followed as both the embodiment and accomplishment of the Mouride principle of *khidmat* (الخدمات), or serving the community. In order to enact this project, other objectives were set, such as: 1) the training of teachers, in line with the training and accreditation of imams – a very ambitious project still underway in France and throughout Europe and the MENA, especially targeting Islamist radicalisation; 2) the creation of research committees; 3) the hosting of touring marabouts in France; and finally 4) a national *hadiya* (هدية), a donation collected from all the Mouride organisations in France and given on behalf of the Federation to the Khalif Généneral once a year.

NFMF is made up of several committees,[7] of which the Scientific Committee is of the most interest here. Its subdivisions are those of Education, Research and Translation; Pedagogy; Islamic School and Coordination. Their mission is to provide the Mouride *dahiras* of France with the necessary educational tools for acquiring an Islamic education and disseminating Bamba's teaching, the Hadiths (الحديث) and the history of the great Sufi masters. The role of the National Scientific Committee is also to facilitate long-distance learning and to harmonise the teaching programmes. It has representatives in each *dahira*, who are responsible for implementing the proposed activities, such as the organisation of the annual meeting for the children of each region. An example of the scientific activities carried out at the local level is the seminar series recently organised by the Islamic Centre of Taverny, of which a case study follows below.

The actions of the committees do not stop at France, as the *talibés'* link with Touba is significantly nurtured by the diasporic community abroad. The borders of the Mouride community have thus expanded, while the spiritual and figurative centre remains in Touba.[8]

Islam and Secularism:
State of the Art, First Case Study

Throughout 2020, the COVID-19 pandemic that has struck the world over, imposing long periods of lockdown and curfews, did not leave France immune, with the result that the country's social, cultural and religious life has continued virtually over the internet, thorough chat rooms, webinars and Zoom meetings. All the while, terrorist attacks carried out at the hands of allegedly Islamist extremists have shaken the country once again with episodes of horrific violence and alarming topicality. The first was the beheading of a schoolteacher, guilty of vilifying the Prophet Mohammed during his classes on the 'freedom of speech' and using the controversial cartoons published by the magazine *Charlie Hebdo*, whose office in Paris had already been the scene of a violent massacre in 2015 for the same reason. A multiple knife attack at a Catholic church in Nice followed, in which three people died and several were wounded. Finally, on 31 October 2020 in Lyon, a priest from an Orthodox church was shot and wounded.

At this very sombre historical time, marked by both health-related and social crises, the MICT has kept up its schedule as best it can and organised a seminar series on Zoom with the title 'Islam et Laïcité: Etat des Lieux'[9] in order to reflect on these issues that are so contentious in France and make the Muslim community as much the victim as the offender. The seminars took place over three weekends, in the format of a round table, hosting several contributors. Every session lasted about two hours. The one that I am presenting here focused on the vexed question of a French Islam. The first speaker introduced the discussion by arguing:

The question of a French Islam is today pre-eminent, one that occupies the media and the political scene at the highest level of the executive and therefore of the French State. Although Islam in France is a very young phenomenon, [and] its first presence only surfaced in the 1970s, the Muslim community now ranges between five to six million people. Those who will constitute the cornerstone of the French Islam came from a modest, rural, illiterate background, little versed in the practice of worship. Their environment was neither politicised nor organised. Islam was nonetheless bound to become plural, as it is made up of Maghrebians, West Africans, Middle Easterners, Europeans and Asians, not to mention the native French people who have converted or the Muslims who have naturalised as French. [It is] A human patchwork that is as much multilingual (e.g. Berber, Asian, African languages etc.) as multicultural and multi-dogmatic, with both Sunnism and Shiism, which clearly create different realities on the ground. Finally, there exist several schools of Islamic law and currents, such as the mystical branches of the various Sufi orders. Furthermore, Islam is multi-ideological: in the last thirty years, political Islam has been supported by the Muslim Brotherhood and Salafist Islam, commonly referred to as Wahhabism, which in turn, have the capacity to integrate other components within their fabric. This plurality poses huge problems of management in France, as it requires a great deal of knowledge and strategy. To this first difficulty is added the colonial heritage, still very present in the collective memory of the Muslims from the ex-colonies, but also of the French Muslims, who continue to be seen as the subjects of France. African Muslims are among the latest migratory groups to settle in France, and they suffer the stigmatisation and misrepresentation that this group generally receives for being both a new migratory group and Muslim. Finally, the handicap of internal conflicts within the multitude of Islamic organisations in France makes the issue of Islam quite complex.

The speaker went on to explain how the question of a French Islam emerged in the 1990s, when a major change in the social fabric occurred in France. A large portion of Muslims became French by both naturalisation and birth,[10] thus acquiring the right to vote and becoming a new public in the political arena. Furthermore, terrorism carried out in the name of Islam accelerated the rationale according to which a home-grown Islam, moulded by Republican values, should free itself of foreign radicalism and thus, under the aegis of the Republic, become safer and more controllable. Nonetheless, the Islamic issue became a hateful and explosive one, difficult to manage. Islamophobic attacks on mosques follow the recurrent terrorist acts as retaliation, amplifying the divide between the wider community and the Muslim one, which is at once victimised and looked down upon with contempt as being impervious to integration. Yet a few facts may still counter this impression: the number of mosques in 1970 did not exceed ten, while today they amount to 2,700, while four hundred more are under construction. Moreover, the principle of *laïcité*, while being areligious, is not anti-religious, and is there to grant freedom of conscience. This is true in France more than in any other country. The speaker reminded the audience that the United States, construed as the example of democracy in the world, has only five million Muslims among its 360 million people, and they have only 1,900 mosques available to them. Comparatively, the same number of Muslims in France, against a national figure of 60 million people, can avail themselves of more than three thousand mosques.

The first Muslim migrants in France, the so-called *bledards*,[11] were little versed in the practice of worship and believed that secularism was the enemy of religion. They were steeped in an Islam of the *bled*, foreign to the French context and its values and ideologies. While they were able to create a new space for the practice of Islam with their meagre intellectual and financial means, they struggled with the new generation. This is why it is crucial, according to the speaker, that Islam today does not focus on worship alone, as it did at the beginning in France. Islam must be able to resonate with the context and time that it inhabits, and reforms are paramount.

A turning point for French Islam occurred through the Tabligh movement, which set out to re-Islamise the African community, especially among Algerians, who, it was argued, had been de-Islamised, possibly due to the long French presence in Algeria. Testimonies recount how the movement would go door-to-door and make the *adhan* in the *foyers*, astonishing the faithful, who had not heard it in years. The migrants' associations have also been a very important lever for the West African migrants and their religious practice, since the Senegalese state did not support them like its Moroccan counterpart did. In addition, those who knew the administration and mastered the French language could reach out to students and create momentum, as well as be propelled into higher roles and status. Migrants' religious associations exist to this day, such as the well-known Fayaka. One former *foyer* resident from Senegal, now a retired man living in Paris with his family, tellingly said:

> Islam did exist at the time; we did not have access to real estate, so we had no choice but praying at home, in our 20 m² of *foyer* room or in the CROUS[12] student rooms. The mosque was just the Great Mosque of Paris, that was it. I was in Marseille, city of cultural mixing, bridging France with the Maghreb, Dakar, Abidjan etc. Year 1985/86: the first Senegalese mosque in Marseille say, when a guy bought a 40 m² store to pray, in the so-called Arab quarter at Cours Belsunce. The person who initiated it served as imam as well. At

the time there were no trained imams, although a few were knowledgeable of the Qur'an. The place was rudimentary, with some mats and no ablution rooms, so we made them at the restaurant next door, and we did not dress traditionally. The arrival of the Left changed everything by allowing migrants to create associations. It was the possibility for foreigners to create their own structures that enabled them to take steps towards their integration and to make demands. So, the small prayer rooms could become mosques, once registered as associations. This transformation gave birth to the Federation of Mosques.

It has been noted that the assassination of President Gamal Abdel Nasser in Egypt by the Free Officers' movement prompted the French government to think it advisable that the migrants come out in the open and form associations after the English way.

Institutional Evolution of a French Islam: Second Case Study

Another poignant Zoom seminar organised by the Islamic Centre of Taverny was on the evolution and role of the Conseil Français du Culte Musulman (CFCM, French Council of the Muslim Faith) for the practice of the Muslim faith. The president of both the Rassemblement des Musulmans de France and of CFCM (2015–18) intervened to sketch a few milestone issues treated by the Council.

From the 1950s up until the 1970s, mosques did not exist, so the faithful practised where possible, sometimes even in unsanitary places. The phenomenon was known as *Islam des caves*, or 'Islam of the cellars'. In 1975, a first circular was issued on the *Carrés Musulmans*,[13] so that French Muslims could be buried in public cemeteries. At the time, the institutions thought of the returnees from Algeria who, although French under the Protectorate, had the status of *indigènes*, so that they were French *with status*, as it were. It was in the 1980s that the public authorities understood the need to establish a dialogue with the Muslim representatives, while religiosity was witnessed to grow with the second generation born to migrant parents. Between 1983 and 1985 the first mosques were founded, together with the Muslim federations, including the Mouride one, as already discussed. In 1983 the Union des Organisations Islamiques de France (UOIF) was created, followed in 1990 by the Conseil d'Orientation et de Réflexion sur l'Islam de France (CORIF), after the troubling 1989 foulard affair. In 1990, the minister Pierre Joxe transformed the Muslim issue into a more sensible religious question, such that the Conseil de Réflexion sur l'Islam en France (CORIF) was formed. This would later give way to the then first minister Nicolas Sarkozy's attempts to create CFCM in 2003, which transformed the Ministry of the Interior into the main reference point for Muslims in France (Frégosi 2005: 101). CFCM[14] was instrumental in incorporating Islam into French territorial policy and preventing foreign funding from interfering with Muslim affairs in France. Since then, the official discourse has sponsored 'the goal of an Islam of France' as opposed to an 'Islam in France' (Laurence and Vaïsse 2006: 138).

In 2002, the Muslim authorities signed a Framework Agreement to commit to respecting the laws and values of the Republic towards the institutionalisation of a French Islam. At this time, there existed twenty-two administrative regions (now thirteen), with regional CFCM bodies (henceforth CRCMs). Given the number of mosques, Île-de-France was divided into three regions: Île-de-France Centre, Île-de-France East (postcodes 77 and 91) and Île-de-France West (postcodes 95 and 78), plus the overseas region of the Reunion Island. The CRCMs were to facilitate the negotiations with the town halls, prefectures and so on, while at the national level, CFCM did so with the Ministries of the Interior and of Agriculture on the issues of halal and ritual slaughter; with those of Foreign Affairs and Tourism on the pilgrimage to Mecca; and with that of National Education on education in high schools. Despite the great deal of work that CFCM has put in since its inception, it is still the object of criticism with regard to its representativity and capacity to grasp the issues that the Muslim community faces on the ground. We heard from the president that:

> Some say that CFCM stands for French Council *Against* the Muslims or for French Council *Couscous Mergez*,[15] rather representing the *bledards* than the new generations. In any case, CFCM has advanced despite everything. An example is the structuring of the Muslim Chaplaincy that was set up in 2005. It is organised by sectors: 1) the Military Chaplaincy under the Ministry of Defence. There are about fifty military chaplaincies that support the soldiers in foreign operations, the OPEX (*Opérations Extérieures*), be that in Chad, Mali, etc.; 2) the Prison Chaplaincy under the Ministry of Justice, with sixty prison chaplaincies throughout France. They play an important role on the question of radicalisation among inmates, which is quite a challenge, and finally; 3) the Hospital Chaplaincy under the Ministry of Health, which supports the elderly or the terminally ill who wish to see an imam; in the event of death, it is in charge of organising the funeral in accordance with the Muslim ritual and of supporting the families.

Thanks to the non-remunerated work of the federations that constitute the CFCM, several thematic commissions were created to work on:

1. the training of imams: the commissions helped recruit imams who would practise in line with the values of the Republic to avoid interference from third countries and pockets of radicalisation. There are now eight training institutes for imams across metropolitan France and the overseas departments (DOM-TOM), with the island of Réunion exporting imams to different countries, including Great Britain;

2. the creation of mosques: CRCMs chaired by the speaker for two terms played an important role as mediators in relation to the question of public cemeteries in the Île-de-France, Seine-et-Marne and Rhone-Alpes, and of the construction of mosques that were previously blocked by the town halls. In 2003, when CFCM was created, there existed 1,300 mosques. That number has doubled in fifteen years;

3. ritual slaughter: CFCM has intensively worked on the halal issue, with support from the three major mosques of Paris, Ivry and Lyon, which had obtained authorisation to certify priests of halal. These mosques signed a charter in March 2016 that enforced the rules to follow throughout the slaughter chain, for both operators and mass distribution, so that a product can be certified as halal;

4. the organisation of *eïds*: this involved an impressive coordination and partnership between the prefectures, the veterinary services and the town halls that host slaughterhouses during the three days of the *eïds*. The slaughter must take place after the *eïds* prayer, under the control of CFCM observers ensuring that the ritual is in strict accordance with the rules of hygiene. Episodes of people carrying out animal slaughter in their houses or garages, like in the old days, are now rare, as this cannot be done nowadays without incurring a fine;

5. the pilgrimage to Mecca: thirty-three thousand pilgrims used to leave France for the *hadji* (حاجي), more than from Muslim countries, although this figure has recently gone down to twenty-five thousand due to works still in progress in Saudi Arabia. Notwithstanding scarce human and financial resources, it is the federations composing the CFCM that finance this.

By way of conclusion, the speaker argued that with the question of radicalisation, CFCM has entered another critical phase, one that President Macron addressed on 17 February 2020 and even more recently on 12 October 2020 at CFCM, and referred to as *Islamic separatism*. This is broadly construed as a phenomenon concerning young people who put themselves in a position of rupture with society. They create a micro-society around a literal interpretation of the Qur'an, without seeking the purpose of these precepts, and departing from the values of the Republic. Hence the vital role of the Islamic Centres, such as that of Taverny, to educate the youth in the values of Islam and respect towards those of the Republic. It was noted in passing that at any event hosted by the MICT, representatives of the town hall are always present.

France is reaffirming its presence on the international scene by promoting *francophonie*, conceived of as a geopolitical world sharing both a common history and heritage, while at the same time acknowledging the cultural, linguistic (Extramiana and Van Avermaet 2010) and religious diversity of its territory, which up until recently was perceived as homogenous (Beauchemin et al. 2016). This is all the more salient with regard to Africa, as the Francophone world lies now, more than ever, in the circulation of both its values and its interlocutors in and from Francophone Africa, an economically, demographically and culturally growing area.

Notes

1. The *khalif* (خليف) is the spiritual leader of the Muslim community, claiming direct succession from the Prophet Mohammed. Since Bamba is conceived of as the *Khadim Rassoul*, servant of the Prophet sent by God, he shares the same status as one of the Prophet's companions, and thus is the initiator of a sacred lineage. Hence the title of khalif for the highest-ranking leader of the Mouride community.
2. *Hizbut* (حزبه) means leadership, while *tarqiyyah* (ترقية) means ascension.
3. A pre-Islamic form of poetry, often translated as 'ode'.
4. CREDI stands for Centre de Recherche d'Étude et de Documentation sur l'Islam (Research Centre for the Study and Documentation of Islam).
5. Muslim associations are extremely composite in nature, due to ethnic and inspirational trends, and generally organised under umbrella federations. The Union of Islamic Organisations of France, created in 1983, includes mainly Moroccans and Tunisians; the National Federation of Muslims of France, created in 1985, has as its base Moroccan Muslim workers and businessmen; the Turkish organisation is made up of four subgroups, ranging from moderate to more radical and extreme right-wing elements (such as the Muslim Union of Cultural Centres of Europe); the Federation of the Muslim Association of Africa, Comoros and the Antilles, which became a French federation in 2000, is confined to the Parisian region; the missionary and community-based movement, Tabligh, established in France in 1970, has split into two subgroups. Moreover, in addition to a plethora of Muslim student associations is the phenomenon of *turuq*, Sufi orders, organised ethnically among the Turkish and Kurdish (the Naqchibandyya and Betachiyya), African (the Tijianyya, Qadriyya and Mouridiyya) and Maghrebian (Tijianyya, Isawiyya and Alawiyya) communities (Diop 2000: 24–25).
6. The MICT was among the signatories of the project, although it now participates in NFMF's initiatives as an invited independent party.

7. The following NFMF committees exist: the Commission Administrative; the Commission Information et Communication; the Commission Administrative et Affaires Juridiques; the Commission Patrimoine; the Commission Scientifique; the Commission Affaires Sociales; the Commission Organisation et Remise Hadiya (هدية).

8. The Social Affairs Committee presides over the managing of this town and its special religious status.

9. 'Islam and Secularism: State of the Art'. All the quotations in both the first and second case study are the author's translations from French, language in which this seminar series on Zoom was held.

10. West African migration to France is now into its third generation.

11. *Bled*, from the Arabic *al balayidan* (البليدان), means 'village' or 'countryside', so *bledard* means 'peasant' or 'countryman'.

12. CROUS is the managing body for student halls.

13. Literally 'Muslim square metres', or plots of land reserved to Muslims in French cemeteries, generally kept separate from the other tombs.

14. The council includes umbrella federations, such as the very conservative Musulmans de France (MDF), ideologically close to the Muslim Brotherhood, and the National Federation of Muslims of France (FMCF), both challenging the dominant Algerian leadership of the Grand Mosque of Paris, whose rector, Dalil Boubakeur (1992–2020), has also been the president of the council (2003–8 and 2013–15).

15. The irony arises from adapting the acronym CFCM into 'Conseil Français *Contre* (instead of Culte) les Musulmans' or into 'Conseil Français *Couscous Mergez*' (instead of Musulmans).

7

French Provision of Health for Migrants

Between Mediation and Misunderstanding

Transcultural Psychiatry and Métissage[1]

The aftermath of the Second World War meant a huge movement of people from the ex-colonies (Collignon 2004) due to the need for a labour force in the reconstruction of France, to care for and assist orphans, refugees and others. Mental health studies began turning their attention towards comparative approaches, namely towards people from different social and cultural backgrounds. In Senegal, Henri Collomb and his team's outstanding work at the Fann Hospital of Dakar was part of this atmosphere that made 'community therapy' become one of the groundbreaking tools of this new transcultural epoch. Still in Senegal, the Ortigues (1984) and Zempleni (1966) attempted to make sense of the culturally framed meaning and expression of psychopathology. Anthropological work moved towards the understanding and description of local understandings of illness and suffering, shifting towards cognitive and semantic approaches (Littlewood 1989). In France, 'ethnopsychiatry reached its apogee with the foundation of the Centre George Devereux, annexed to the University Paris8' (Sargent and Larchanché 2009b: 101). Devereux's school inaugurated a new way of doing psychiatry by combining clinical practice, research and teaching. Tobie Nathan, his student, espoused his teacher's approach in relating anthropology and psychiatry to one another as ethno-psychiatry (Nathan 1994). Nonetheless, his theory and clinical practice have recently fallen under the criticism of both anthropologists and clinicians, who accuse him of carrying out 'folk therapy'. First in line is renowned French anthropologist Didier Fassin. It is impossible not to consider the latter's extremely prolific work when addressing medical anthropology in Paris, in particular with regard to West African migrants' healthcare (Fassin 1992, 2009). Implicit in both Fassin's (1999, 2000) critique and in the clinical work carried out with migrants by associations like Migrations et Santé is the refusal to think of the migrant's adaptation (after migration) as a one-way process, that is, as the migrant's reintegration into their own community.

According to Littlewood and Lipsedge (2004), what is at stake in migrants' healthcare is precisely the affirmation of power – of the dominant group – over those excluded from it, that is, the migrants and subdominant groups. This may occur in various guises, from blatant racism to obtuse reductionism in therapy, making of one's culture one's exclusive fate. The authors criticise the possibility of a specific migrant's psychopathology, although they argue that the harsher the accommodation process, the likelier psychopathologies are to be induced. In this sense, illness is a complex experience entailing as much societal (of both the sending and receiving countries) as individual meaning-making, beyond the specificity of the physical disease (Rivers 1923; Kleinman 1980, 1988), which intercultural therapy (Kareem and Littlewood 2020) and an anthropological understanding address. In Europe, and France in particular, healthcare for minority groups has usually been associated with social rights and, more specifically, with the right to receive healthcare, regardless of one's status (legal or illegal migrant). Fassin astutely remarks that social, political and anthropological debates have gone closer to the universalism of the *droit commun* and of human rights, in the opposite direction of the initial fights that advocated the recognition of migrants' rights based on their cultural difference.[2]

In France, the concept of *métissage* is also in use both in clinical practice (Moro et al. 2006; Moro 2002) and as an anthropological orientation to understand people whose background is diverse in terms of origin and culture (Laplantine and Nouss 2011).

Between Malaise and Marginalisation

At Foyer93, those who do not have a job spend most of their time idly, hanging about in the court and at the cafe or going out in the neighbourhood, while hoping for something to 'unblock', such as obtaining a permit or finding a job. In a similar situation to these individuals, generally in their thirties and forties, are the elders, who have retired and spend their time in the court, chatting away or simply sitting in chairs next to one another, looking around passively. Younger residents get by working in scaffolding, at conveyer belts in factories and in other menial jobs, even when illegal, as businesses take advantage twice over of their status by underpaying them and by saving on social benefits (personal communication).

The elders share their rooms with other residents of their age. They often have no family members at Foyer93 because these have either found accommodation in Paris and moved on, because they have finally returned home or – most of all – because the elders have not been able to guarantee the arrival of younger male family members in France. Their isolation within the *foyer* and from the family, and not least from their women in Kayes, weakens them vis-à-vis the other residents, those who are younger and those who are better connected. They receive little mercy or consideration: their opinion does not count much in the general managing of Foyer93, nor do their needs or complaints (e.g. about the noise coming from neighbouring rooms or about the *délégués*' work). Instead, they are tagged non-euphemistically as those who rant or uselessly moan. They drag themselves from their rooms to the court, at times indulging a little in the canteen, while the cafe is off limits, since it is too undignified a place for them. Although the cafeteria does not serve alcohol, the elders think that good Muslims should not attend bars. As a consequence, the cafe is crowded only with young and middle-aged residents. In the rooms, they lie down and relax, or pray even beyond the set times of the ritual prayers; those who have a TV watch it. Hours go by that way. Elders do not venture much outside Foyer93, as the court provides them with the impression of being outdoors anyway. Their lack of mobility – which is similar to that of all of the residents, inasmuch as most find it impossible to either move out of Foyer93 or to return home – is reflected in their fixed gazes and lack of conversation, besides the random outbursts of bitterness directed towards their perceived rivals, be they the *délégués*, 'who talk for nothing', or the 'noisy youth' and 'the French'. Simaga, the iron-maker, told me that back home, people who stay in particular corners all the time are dangerous, because they can cast 'bad influences' on you, or *sort jetté*, but he was quick to add that this was not the case of the elders in the *foyer*, because they are 'innocuous', which can easily be construed as being powerless. Nobody fears them, or even considers them. The elders' isolation and reclusion have diminished their status, as they are otherwise highly respected within Malian and West African society, where they occupy a central position in the traditional and family-centred scale of values.

As previously discussed, most of those who moved to France in the 1970s thought that their spouses should remain in the homeland or risk becoming 'impolite'. This way of thinking is not as quaint as it would appear, since Muslim women in France are the object of a political discourse based on secularism that directly (for instance through the law banning the hijab in public) or indirectly encourages them to attack their men's authority and, more generally, Islam. The principle of *laïcité* also opposes Islam on the grounds of feminist arguments, as the only way left to Muslim women to 'free themselves'. By choice or circumstance, the elders have responded to state interventionism and control by keeping at bay any interference: the state can do little to their women when they are not in France, nor to themselves if they keep together as a community. Although to some extent this strategy has proved satisfactory – Foyer93 has yet to be demolished and the community is still there; their women and children are still 'protected' by the family in Kayes and their financial input from France – they have paid a costly price. Over the years and through their repeatedly postponed returns, these men have had a surrogate role as heads of the family, and often one that is limited to the possibility of sending money. They have transformed Foyer93 into their home, while juggling their positions in the family from afar. The experience of the residents in their forties, who are out of work and often without a residency permit, is akin to that of the elders, increasingly isolating, frustrating and angering them. One day, I found one resident in tears because he was unable to send what was due for his son's school fees and clothes. He vented his frustration against France and its migration policy. The ageing of the migrant population at Foyer93 suggests a failure of the *foyer* system, which rather than providing a gateway to wider society has morphed into a trap.

Postcolonial, Islamic and Community-Bound Representations of Affliction

As Keller (2007: 4) pointed out, colonial psychiatry was 'at different periods ... less a weapon in the arsenal of colonial racism than it was a tool for the emancipation of the colonised, a discipline in crisis and a mechanism for negotiating the meaning of difference for republican citizenship'. The author reminds us of how, from the orientalist tradition to postcolonial literature, Islam and insanity have often been associated. According to the former, the Muslim world emerged as the land of insanity, which justified the French settlement in North and West Africa as the guardians of order and health, through military force and asylums.

Postcolonial studies attribute to colonial brutality both the state of chaos of the colonised countries and the mental distress of the subjects, as elucidated by anthropologist and forefather of psychiatry Frantz Fanon (1963, 1967), who addressed in particular the effects of French colonial violence in Algeria.

Within the Islamic tradition, the jinns, humanlike spirits, live a parallel life to that of humans. Some troublesome jinns are said to attack people and interfere with their lives, creating troubles of the mind and misfortune. They are commonly thought to inhabit forests or deserted places. The jinns are mentioned in the Qur'an (Sura 72), and variously in the Hadith of the Prophet, as having been created from the 'smokeless flames of fire', from which Satan, *shaytan* (الشيطان), is also thought to originate. Interestingly, from the Arabic root of the noun jinn stem the words *maynuun* (مجنون), mad, and *janna* (الجنة), paradise, also reflected in the Soninké distinction between *waxanté*, madness, and *jinebena*, the attack of the jinns requiring traditional healing. The African cultural landscape is dotted with the figures of traditional and religious healers, who are able to connect the human sphere to the supernatural realm to tackle its effects in nature. As previously noted, according to Islamic cosmogony, divinity emanates from God in different forms of ontological realities, or *ayat* (آيات).

The association of illness and health with the same source, which is ultimately spiritual, is particularly salient. Illness and health unfold in mediation, or through a process of negotiation with the spiritual realm, which implies the essentially non-psychotic nature of the possessed (Beneduce 2002: 87). Hence the puzzlement of the clinician in discerning the interaction between culturally rooted statements regarding alleged attacks by the jinn, as reported by Muslim patients, and episodes of illness that fall within conventional medicine. Indeed, some patients only recover after resorting to traditional healing (Khalifa 2005). According to clinical studies of psychopathologies carried out in West Africa (Sylla et al. 2001; Corin et al. 1993), isolation appears to be the main marker of the inception of madness among the Senegalese and Bambara groups, where descriptions revolve around ideas of a non-integrated self – *fatò*, in Bambara. Therefore, 'being calm' and 'not answering properly' denote the boundary between sanity and insanity. Among the Soninkés, while withdrawal indicates the presence of a problem, generally associated with depressive states possibly linked to professional deception (Corin et al. 1993: 142, 147), confrontation, disputes and bizarre appearances and behaviour testify to one's *waxanté*, courage and dynamism being characteristics of the Soninké 'sane' identity (ibid.: 151). Mental illness in this context is thus a kind of extravagance, as opposed to the Senegalese and Malian milieus, whereby it implies impoliteness and aggressiveness.

My respondents addressed the subject of illness and affliction, and its causality and effects, in terms of human destiny. Affliction, superseding illness, takes shape in many ways, from an attack of the jinn to witchcraft and even an encounter with a negative person. Muslims and Non-Muslims undergo the same suffering, physical and mental, but act upon it differently, since the former ascribe their condition to mystical agents whose agency is part of a divine plan. Because the Qur'an states that Muslims are compelled to heal themselves by any possible means, my respondents believe that in the face of illness, both mainstream medicine and traditional healing are valid. They define themselves as the generation of change, between the receiving country and the country of origin, receptive to both worlds, especially in their health-seeking behaviour. They do not despise Western doctors in relation to their marabouts: they find the former useful for treating physical ailments, and the latter better placed to deal with troubles of the mind, since these are thought to entail the domain of the spirits. The distinction between marabout and healer is one that separates the domain of *baraka*, grace – the mystical power channelled by God – from that of *lasrar* (لاسرار), secret – the magical knowledge that can be used to harm people. As previously noted, in my respondents' view, this ontological complexity adds to the confusion in Europe regarding who is a marabout, a healer or one who practises witchcraft, all of whom are equally seen as synonymous with charlatans. Simply put, while marabouts provide blessings through prayers, healers[3] protect you by ritually summoning the jinns and by producing amulets and protective objects containing extracts from the Qur'an, such as necklaces and leather belts.

Pitt-Rivers (1992) noted the remarkable absence of anthropological literature on the subject of grace, with an exception made for the works of Mauss (2002) and Lévi-Strauss (1949), for whom, respectively, 'the concepts of gift and exchange entail that of gratuitous reciprocity, the cement which holds any society together' (Pitt-Rivers 1992: 218). Divine grace is solicited by sacrifices, since 'the offering invites a return-gift of grace, the friendship of God' (ibid.: 223). In contrast to the relatively scarce literature on the subject of grace, the concept of *baraka* enjoys broad attention in Islamic Studies. Werbner (2003: 250) talks of a 'symbolic complex of blessing', in which *barkat* (البرکات) is only one term among several that specifically refer to a particular form of saintly power, which is not only used for healing and exorcism. In this sense, 'it is a generic Islamic term for divine blessing. *Barkat* imbues objects, such as the salt given by the Sufi saint, with the power of procreation, life, fertility and so on' (ibid.: 251). Furthermore, '*Barkat* is magic and contagious. This means that the Sufi saint is charged physically with *barkat*), which explains why he is constantly mobbed by devout followers, endangering his life in their attempts to touch him' (ibid.: 252). *Barkat* can thus be transmitted metonymically as well as metaphorically to things, 'crystallising embodied connections between a sacred centre and its extended peripheries' (Werbner and Basu 1998: 13). In the Sufi milieus, *khalwat* (خلوة) is another propitiatory ritual practised to seek guidance and inspiration from God. This is a very old and well-known Islamic tradition, which sees the aspirant believer withdraw in meditation with their marabout as a guide for forty days, during which they resort to *istikhar* (الإستخار),[4] a consultation prayer used to stimulate premonitory dreams, anticipating God's will.[5]

Working with the Jinns

During my fieldwork in Paris, I met Drame, a healer to whom I was introduced by community members at Foyer93. He held his divination sessions at his house in Barbès. Drame underlined that his clientele belonged to his own circle of people, a proof of sorts of his talent and renown, which in fact should not normally need to be advertised. As he put it, those who stand at metro stations publicising themselves as miracle workers are nothing of the kind, and they spoil the image of the 'real ones' in the minds of the French. If someone is a good healer, people in the community know, as the information is spontaneously passed on and circulated. Drame is also said to confront *liguééy*, sorcery in Wolof. People consult him when they think that somebody, or the jinns, either in Africa or France, is trying to harm them, and when they wish to achieve or change something in their lives. In fact, problems for which one may seek the healer's intervention may vary from an attack of a jinn to alcoholism, infidelity, sexual impotence and 'wrong' marital matches. The last time I visited him, a woman from a maraboutic family[6] was there to ask Drame to 'break' her son's relationship with a girl of griot descent. Although with migration, caste affiliation has become less meaningful due to social mobility and similarity of status within the migrant working class, marrying into a lower caste is still disapproved of. Overall, the ritual implies the use of the *hatim*, a grid associating a numerological system to letters written in Arabic, corresponding to the name of the person involved (or other personal details). The resulting number provides a formula that is then used for protection. One of these, called *hatim of Souleymane* (see Table 7.1), is deemed useful for healing all kinds of illnesses. Translated from the Arabic, it reads: 'a marabout is working to take you', meaning that the healer is casting away the jinn. Other grids apply different letters, which therefore result in different numerical combinations and formulas.

Drame summons *rauhan* and *khudan*, jinns of a kind, to guide him during divination. In his view, not all practitioners have the power to deal with these spirits, since they only associate with men of the highest spirituality, virtue and knowledge of the Qur'an. The intervention of the guiding spirit may in fact fail to occur if the practitioner has misbehaved or failed to carry out his prayers. In this case, he should praise the spirits and gain their intervention by asking forgiveness. The Surat Al-Jinna (سورة الجنة) – the seventy-second in the Qur'an and the twenty-eighth of the Revelation[7] – is useful for this purpose. The jinns are therefore crucial, since they are the practitioner's allies, without whom he could not operate. The success of the practitioner's intervention lies in his moral standing, so that good, as opposed to evil, is not only a Muslim principle of behaviour, but embodied spirituality attained through practice, a source of healing power that is put to use for the good of the community. During divination, all the agents involved undergo a test. Reparation thus entails mediation in different realms, where what is at stake is not only the resolution of the specific problem, but also a wider equilibrium that needs rebalancing.

The ontological reality of the jinns is beyond time and space, so their attack is construed as an 'interference' (Taneja 2018) with our world that can take place at any time and anywhere; it may be caused by jealousy or love (the jinns may favour specific people) or by anger (one may have inadvertently crossed or stepped on them). In fact, they live among us in spiritual form, or by taking on the shapes of humans, animals, aspects of nature or even alcoholic beverages (Dorris 2011). There can be benign as well as troublesome jinns, and Muslim and non-Muslim ones. They are thought to be responsible for one's misfortune, a wide category that encompasses health problems (e.g. premature birth, illness, mental distress), the loss of a loved one (through death or the end of a relationship) and various other forms of grievance (e.g. lack of respect, fights in the family or dishonour). They are said to enter people's houses at dusk, so it is good practice to shut the windows and carry out the *maghrib* (المغرب), the compulsory evening prayer.

The pantheon of the jinns are extremely varied, ranging from the phenomenon of the *rab* (رب) in Senegal to that of the *koma* cult in Mali. The former has been thoroughly studied by both Zempleni (1966) and the Ortigues (1984) in relation to the Wolof, Serer and Peul ethnic groups. The *rab* is a spirit believed to coexist with an individual through-

Table 7.1. Hatim of Souleymane. © D. Accoroni.

د	ج	ب	ا
d = 4	j = 3	b = 2	a = 1
ح	ز	و	ه
h = 8	z = 7	w = 6	He = 5
ل	ط	ى	ء
L = 30	ta = 20	i = 10	Tua = 9
ع	ص	ن	م
ain = 70	s = 60	n = 50	m = 40
ر	ق	ض	ف
r = 200	q = 100	da = 90	f = 80
خ	ث	ت	س
Kh = 600	tha = 500	ta = 400	s = 300
ش	غ	ظ	ذ
Ch = 1,000	Rahine = 900	zha = 800	dh = 700

out their life, typically a male ancestor who lives on in the family. Zempleni highlighted the importance of discerning the *rab* through the ritual called *ndepp* in Wolof. Once the *rab* has been determined and given a place in the family lineage, it is then linked to the family altar, the *samp*, to become *tuur*, an identified spirit. Normally, identification results in the resolution of the possession state or remission of the illness, or both (Lambek 1981). Regarding the latter cult, in the Mandinka mountains of Mali, a circle of initiated people, the *koma*, linked to the jinns, are responsible for circumcising male youths and for protecting the community from witchcraft and foreign intrusions (Zobel 1996). They are called *nyamakalaw* in Bambara, or men of knowledge, and they comprise those working at the forge, *numuw*; the griots, *jeliw*; the specialists in the Muslim tradition, *funew*, and the craftsmen, *garankew*. The presence of the *forgerons* at Foyer93 shows that migration involves individuals across the whole social stratification. Leaders of the *koma* are alternatively called *moriw*, marabouts, and *soma*, 'priest-witches'. They are the nobles of the *koma*, and are able to fabricate objects of power, heal and make sacrifices to the jinns. Divination rituals are carried out by the *warada* and are associated with 'visible trance states' (ibid.: 645). They are able to communicate with the jinns by using the Qur'an and prayer beads. The *koma* do not think that the jinns are incorporated into the human body, but that they are just visible, and moreover that they sustain social relations with the *moriw*, who summons them during the ritual. This tradition, *komajinne*, is considered a form of paganism (locally called animism), but it is not in contradiction with Islam. The representatives of both traditions cooperate and endorse each other, by paying one another visits or, as with the *koma*, by limiting aspects of the ritual that may conflict with Islam, like the use of masks. The Muslim jinns, as opposed to the *komajinne*, are understood to 'possess the individual, inflicting pain and misfortune' (ibid.: 647). The knowledge of the secrets and functioning of the *koma* appears to be non-systemic, 'depending on having used protective medicines and on the possession of powerful objects and secrets' (ibid.: 642). This characteristic is shared by other healing and Sufi traditions, as Brenner (1985) showed, while Last (1981, 1988) sophisticatedly argued that not knowing can be part of a 'medical culture' (1981: 387).

The residents of Foyer93 endorse healers for their skills, but most often because of what they represent: their common tradition, language, identity and needs. Marabouts and healers belong to the same milieu as their clients and experience in the same way the difficulties of settling in the big city. For many residents, obtaining a residence permit or avoiding a police check can be reason enough to visit a healer. Whether or not the healers are trustworthy or considered less powerful than those left in the home country, my respondents' belief system remains unquestioned and its practice unperturbed. Marabouts and healers guarantee the marginal yet vital space of hope that things can be manipulated and turned in their favour, and that the spiritual realm, as opposed to the law, can still satisfy their demands as human beings.

In conclusion, notwithstanding the endeavours of French transcultural psychiatry to alleviate migrants' afflictions and to bridge the gap that exists between wider French society and first-generation migrants, it still cannot extend its medical provision to people like the residents of Foyer93. This possibility is already hindered, as they are increasingly more conscious of the fact that what France offers is not designed for them, who are socially marginal. They sense that French healthcare, premised on a secular and disenchanted standpoint, is ultimately detached from their most immediate needs and spirituality. This points to the need for a form of mediation that would see them and their interlocutors (healers, associations and religious leaders) as being at the centre of the process, not unlike Collomb's pioneering community-based project (previously mentioned), which proved successful. Marabouts and healers still give migrants the guarantee of being listened to, understood and fortified in their spiritual and social quest. Thus, among West African migrants, the former's role flourishes in the wider setting of health and in the realm of divination and anti-sorcery, which reinforces the belief in *baraka* as the migrants' way of understanding the world and dealing with it.

Notes

1. Parts of this chapter have been used in a revised form in my peer-reviewed article 'Transcultural Psychiatry and the French Provision of Health for Migrants: Between Mediation and Misunderstanding'. 2017. *Transtext(e)s Transcultures* 跨文本跨文化: *Journal of Global Cultural Studies* 12. https://doi.org/10.4000/transtexts.991.
2. Migrants can in fact claim residency rights, if they can prove that they can only receive treatment in France. It is currently being debated whether undocumented migrants, who have stayed in France for at least three years and worked for at least one, should be legalised by their employers ('Zoom', 2021. *Le CGT Ensemble* 143: 2).
3. A Muslim healer, however, is generically also called a 'marabout'. In the text, I distinguish between 'healer' and 'marabout' for clarity.
4. See http://www.islamicacademy.org/html/Dua/How_to_do_Istakhara.htm (accessed 7 September 2020).
5. This prayer consists of two *rakas* (ركعاس), cycles of the prayer Nafl Salat (نفل صلاة), interspersed with different suras followed by a *duha* (دعاء), prayer of praise to Allah and by salutations to God's grace. In the first *raka*, one should recite the suras Al-Fatiha (الفاتحة) and Al-Kafirun (الكافرون); in the second, Al-Fatiha is followed by the sura Al-Ikhlas (الاخلاص).
6. Maraboutic families stand for the traditional religious elite and hold great prestige. The griots, who are still the repositories of the Soninké oral tradition (as previously discussed), are nonetheless of lower status.
7. The suras are ordered in the Qur'an by length, and therefore do not follow the chronological order in which they appeared historically. This is why Muslims refer in the first case to the standard order, while in the latter to the 'Suras of the Revelation'. Accordingly, they produce different counts.

Conclusion

Global World, Blocked Migrants

My analysis has focused primarily on the Soninké community from the region of Kayes, living in a *foyer* in the Seine-Saint-Denis department of the Île-de-France region. The *foyers* can be said to be peculiar to France, since nowhere else in Europe do migrants live in similar accommodation. The *foyers* were conceived to host the first Algerian migrants during the reconstruction of France, in the aftermath of the Second World War. The new generation of migrants are generally hosted in the same old *foyers* as in the past. No maintenance work or security measures have been implemented since. These *foyers* are commonly referred to as *foyers-taudis*, that is, slums. Foyer93 is no exception.[1] Since the residents themselves facilitate their family members' arrival in France, other non-community members are barred access. The villages of origin thus determine the composition of the *foyers*, resulting in quite a homogenised crowd, often speaking the same language – in this case Soninké, although Bambara may be used, being the currency language in Mali.

Migration to France is no longer temporary, as the second-generation migrants testified as early as the 1980s (see the Algerian *Beur* movement), so the *foyers* themselves have turned into life-long residences for male migrants, where women and children, that is, these people's families, are absent. This has engendered first the ageing of the residents at Foyer93, now a concern for the associations working on the ground for migrants' health and well-being, and secondly a new migratory pattern.

While the return home is less and less viable (due to both the obligation to reside in France to receive pension schemes and to their illegality, from which it is increasingly difficult to escape), allegiance to the village is gradually changing in meaning.

The French state and medical programmes hint at the idea that the methods demonstrated by Devereux are outdated, such that to look back to one's own community for intra-aid and reference – *communautarisme* – cannot be pursued in France, as the principles of *laïcité* and Republicanism oppose this drive in a fundamental way. All the same, my respondents' answers seem subtler than that: their health-seeking behaviour results from a combination of different options available to them, from French medical care to traditional healing, while they find support and comfort in the community life that Foyer93, notwithstanding its internal divisions and clashes, still offers. The elderly, who need particular medical attention, follow the same pattern as the youth: they resort to medical treatment at a very late stage. Nonetheless, a generational change is underway, whereby although the village is still at the centre of the residents' migratory project (in terms of remittances and development projects), it no longer determines their life expectations. While the older migrants decided to keep their spouses back in the village, their younger counterparts mix their lives at Foyer93 with their activities outside of it. What is new is that this is considered the way forward, unlike in the past, when settling in France was considered a betrayal of village allegiance.

Nonetheless, ever since Muslim migrants first settled in Europe, the question of practising Islam has remained central, and even grown. Prayer rooms started appearing in the *foyers*, and today, Islam has become the second religion of France; with it, a national goal has arisen to transform it into a French *affaire*, the Mouride Islamic Centre of Taverny being an exemplar. However, especially following the string of terrorist attacks in Europe at the hands of radicalised Muslims, migration rules have toughened all over the world, and Muslim diasporic communities have had to renegotiate their loyalty to the nations that host them. In dealing with Muslim migrants, each country has addressed the topic of integration and Islam, often as overlapping agendas, whereby Muslim practice has become the grounds on which to validate or invalidate Muslims. In France in particular, the debate about the integration of the Muslim population, both migrant and French, while certainly not new, has intensified. The suspicion under which Muslims are kept is expressed through the exclusionary policies that aim at reducing their proximity, their visibility and, by and large, the successful insertion into society of newcomers to France. Examples abound, prominent ones being the foulard affair and the concentration of the migrant community in specific areas, such as the banlieues and the *foyers*. It also appears that the French national focus on *francophonie* contributes to establishing enduring links in Africa rather than promoting softer migration rules or better conditions for migrants in France, which might stimulate greater undesired migration flows. Thus, health projects, which are expensive and difficult to carry out (both in France and in West Africa), are few and are only sporadically funded: budgetary cuts and the constant demand for the standardisation of procedures make the lives of associations working for migrants' healthcare very short.

Final Considerations

This book is intended to be a contribution to Migration, Politics of Healthcare, Religious and Francophone Studies, in that it examines the accommodation process and well-being of male Soninké migrants from Kayes, Mali, living in a *foyer* in Paris. Anthropological studies have generally focused on the role of young people in affecting changes in traditional norms and behaviours within and outside their milieu. In my study, those young migrants are now the elderly of Foyer93, who brought about an inexorable change by initiating the first *international migrations*. My study has revealed how the residents have commenced a process of detachment from their villages of origin – contrary to classic understandings of rural – urban mobility in Africa (Geschiere 2005; Geschiere and Gugler 1998; Gugler 2002), which saw the return and the link to the homeland as an irrefutable fact – while pointing out the constraints within which this community is left to live and create wealth for themselves and their families in Kayes.

The knot that remains to be unravelled is how France manages migration, together with the difficult issue of Islam and the Muslims. The loyalty to the nation demanded of the generations of children born to migrant parents cannot fail to be undermined by the way that their fathers and forefathers were received in France in the first place. The problem lies in the past more compellingly than it does in the future. People at Foyer93 are in limbo, since both going back home and moving into mainstream life in France is now impossible. Transnational ideas of migration, showing successful migrants building their and their villages' futures through movement, cannot grasp the current context. In fact, these migrants are fundamentally trapped at the margins of society, with little hope of escaping them, since moving out of the *foyers* would entail the end of the community and its internal networks of aid and support, and thus the end of their only safe base in Paris.

Ideas of gradual assimilation by proximity, that is, of integration as an outcome of successive migrant generations coming to France, have proved to be misplaced. The distance between the Soninké minority group and the wider French society has increased. While essentialising portrayals of migrants depict them as the promoters of their villages' development, to which they are primarily oriented, only a few could confirm this model at Foyer93. The majority of the residents live very idiosyncratically, their desire to improve their own lives in France frustrated by their families' demands and by the increasing expectations, both French and Malian, about the future of the villages. In addition, the hypothesis according to which the overcrowding of Foyer93 would eventually impair village solidarity by stopping other community members from entering has been disproved. The trend is one of greater male migration to France and to the *foyers* in particular, which have reached a point of exhaustion, with an increase of independent female migration as well, spurred by the 1986 Pasqua Law restricting family reunions. The feminisation of migration has become an inspiring new subtopic in the field of Migration Studies, while until recently female migration was only a shadow of its male counterpart. Returnees are outnumbered by those who have decided to stay, settling down in the *foyers* or making their accommodation between the *foyer* and elsewhere in Paris. The *foyers* are now the new permanent homes of the Soninké migrants, in which the elder generations are ageing. The ultimate destination is no longer the village, but Paris itself, where the family will eventually live. The lexicon too has changed: migrants now 'visit home' if their legal status is cleared, but permanent returns are very unlikely. Migrants are cloistered within the limits of the community in Paris, if not of the *foyer* itself – a retreat constituted through fear of state interventionism and pragmatism. In this context, tradition and Islam intervene to validate dynamics that already exist or that are chosen by the residents.

In sum, theirs is a very stable experience in Paris, and it has been so since the beginning of the twenty-first century. The loyalty of the Muslim minority groups to the village of origin and to Islam now has a different meaning, as the Mouride faithful in the Île-de-France region show: they have detached from the administration in Senegal, while they draw on an Islamic universalism intended to counter the overreaching French secularism that undermines them as individuals. I have also shown how the institutionalisation of Islam has marked a threshold for the Muslim community of France, which now constitutes the second religion of the country, with almost six million faithful. Their legislative commissions advance the community's representation through the Muslim federations that compose the CFCM, and several issues, such as the creation of mosques, the ritual slaughter and the *eïds*, have been successfully addressed. The goal of a French Islam, although not attained once and for all, seems to have advanced a long way from the Islam that was practised in cellars by the first migrants, newly arrived from the ex-colonies to France.

Note

1. While I was writing this book, Foyer93 has finally closed its doors, following the increasing degradation of the site. Plans for its relocation, housing fewer people (as feared by the residents all along) albeit in better conditions, are underway.

Glossary

Arabic, Soninké and Wolof Words

Barkat: divine gift; this is generally referred to as *baraka* and attributed to the saint (*wali*) due to his proximity to God. *Barkat* can broadly signify good luck, as well as the power of the saints. Such power can metonymically be endowed to things, so that even the latter can 'have' *baraka*.

Bidan: an Arabo-Berber ethnic group found in the Hodh and Sahel areas.

Bled: 'village' or 'countryside', from the Arabic *al balayidan* (البلايدان).

Daara: in Senegal, Mouride communities of single men (*takder*) who work the fields and learn the Qur'an under the direction of the marabout or his representative (*diawrigne*). The *daaras* still exist, even though urban *dahiras* and the *talibés*' networks are now the main features of Mouridism, both in Senegal and in the diaspora.

Dahira: an urban Mouride circle that corresponds to the second phase of the Mouride history, when the community migrated to urban centres. The faithful felt the need to create networks, affiliating the *talibés* of the same marabout or simply those wishing to pray together in the same neighbourhood.

Dar al-harb: the land where Islam is absent, as opposed to **dar al-Islam**, the land of Islam.

Dhikr: remembrance of God by the ritual repetition of His Names. The *dhikr* ritual can be chanted or pronounced. Some Sufi orders carry out the *dhikr* by pronouncing the names 'internally', in meditation (*fiqr*), others by complementing the meditation with music and dances. This Sufi ritual is spread throughout the world. *Kourel* is a Wolof term designating a particular way of performing the *dhikr*.

Duha: a supererogatory praising prayer.

Eïd-el-fitr and eïd-el-kébir: the two Muslim celebrations marking respectively the end of Ramadan (Muslim ritual fasting) and the commemoration of Abraham's sacrifice. The latter involves the ritual slaughter of a ram. In Senegal, eïd-el-kébir is referred to as *tabaski*.

Griot (fem. griotte): in West Africa, the griots were a caste of people who used to chant praises and the genealogy of important families by heart. This tradition is still kept alive, such that the griots of renowned griot families are now community singers, contributing to festive and religious occasions with their chants.

Hadiya: a donation given to the marabout as a tangible sign of gratitude.

Hadith (pl. ahādīth; lit. 'discussion'): the collection of narrations concerning the words and deeds of the Prophet Mohammed.

Hijab (lit. 'covering'): stands for the Muslim female practice of modesty, or way of dressing. The *hiqab* is the covering of the body and head. The burqa is the full covering of the body, head and face. The use of the term 'hijab' to refer to head coverings (the headscarf) is recent.

(Salat al-)Istikhar (the 'guidance prayer'): understood to stimulate premonitory dreams, anticipating God's will. It should be followed by a *duha* (also preceded and followed by salutations to God's grace), and ablutions before sleeping. The *istikhar* prayer is resorted to when a choice is to be made or when embarking on something new. This is one form of divination.

Ka gumme: Soninké leader of the *ka*, the productive units made of different households of the same lineage. Work is divided between primary and personal fields, or *saluma*.

Kafir (pl. kuffār, from the root k-f-r, lit. 'to cover up'): the one who rejects God, an infidel or pagan, but also an unbeliever in Islamic doctrine. These terms have become derogatory; thus, *kafir* is now generally translated as the more nuanced 'non-Muslim'.

Khadim (lit. 'server') Rassoul (lit. 'the one sent by God', meaning the Prophet): the saint who has been granted by Allah, for their purity and faith, the position of being at the service of the Prophet, so as to become like one of the latter's historical companions.

Khalif Général: the head of the Mouride brotherhood, whose headquarters are based in Touba (Senegal), the sacred town of the Mouride *talibés*. Its mosque is also where Cheick Amadou Bamba M'Backé's tomb is located.

Khalwat (lit. 'solitude'): Sufi spiritual withdrawal, traditionally of forty days, during which a disciple practises extensive spiritual exercises under the direction of a master.

Koma cult: in the Mandinka mountains of Mali, the *koma* are a circle of initiated people linked to the jinns. They are responsible for guarding the group from foreign intrusions, for circumcising male youths and for protecting the community from the powerful witchcraft of women. The jinns of the *koma* cult are called *komajinne*.

Kourel: a chant that serves as a vessel for trance.

Liguééy (lit. 'work'): Wolof term also used to indicate 'sorcery'.

Magal: Mouride commemoration of Bamba's departure to exile in Gabon (September 1895).

Mande: a group comprising the Bambara and Mandinka ethnic groups.

Marabout (murâbit, pl. murâbitûn) or cheick: a term used to identify a spiritual leader, often at the head of a Sufi lodge (*zawiya*), of which he is the initiator or whose teaching he is bound to perpetuate (as *muqaddam*, religious authority).

Mouridiyya (from *mouridoullah*, lit. 'aspirant to God'): a Sufi branch of Islam, founded in Senegal by Cheick Amadou Bamba M'Backé (1855–1927). The Mourides are the faithful of the order.

Mujaddid (lit. 'renovator'): a person who appears at the turn of every century of the Islamic calendar to revive Islam and restore it to its pristine purity. A *mujaddid* might be a saint (*wali*).

Qutb: the most eminent position in the hierarchy of the saints: also means 'pole'.

Raka: the complete cycle of prayer, consisting of 1) a standing position, 2) genuflection (*ruko*), 3) prostration (*sudjût*) and 4) a sitting position (*djuluss*). The morning prayer (*subha*) consists of two *rakas*, the evening prayer (*salat al-maghreb*) of three and the others (*zuhr*, *asr* and *icha*) of four.

Sadaqa (pl. sadaqat): Alms, often in the form of animal sacrifice, given to avert misfortune. This is also used as a general term for donation.

Sas: Wolof term for 'self-taxation', which is differentiated from *hadiya*, the donation given to the marabout as a tangible sign of gratitude.

Salafyya: militant Islam, generally referred to as 'radical Islam'. It originated in Egypt as a reformist movement opposed to European colonial rule and advocated the rational application of God's commandments in the pursuit of general welfare. The movement also intended to modernise the Muslim world by catching up with the technologies of the West.

Serin (lit. 'master') Touba (holy town of the Mourides): refers to Cheick Amadou Bamba M'Backé, the founder of the Mouridiyya and of Touba, the sacred town of the Mourides. The latter hosts what is now the second greatest mosque in West Africa.

Silsila-baraka: the saint's lineage, which supposedly inherits the saint's *baraka* and is thus entitled to the leadership of the community of faith.

Sunna (pl. sunan, lit. 'custom' or 'usual practice'): in Muslim usage, the sayings of the Prophet Muhammad as recorded in the Hadiths.

Tabligh: a transnational religious movement that was revived in 1926 by Muhammad Ilyas al-Kandhlawi in India. It supports the idea of a renovated Islam, not in the form of 'traditional custom', but rather in that of a globalised Islam.

Tafakkur ('act of deliberation', 'pondering'): the first step into Islam, which is 'submission' to this truth, and thus the first obligation of a Muslim.

Tahaqouq: realisation of the Divine nature of the world, as part of the Sufi mystical acquisition of the divine truth, haqiqa.

Talibé: Arabic term meaning disciple or student learning the Qur'an.

Tarbiya: the esoteric science dedicated to the formation of the spirit through the purification of the soul (*ishan*) against the temptations of bodily desires (*nafs*).

Tariqa (pl. turuq): a Sufi order.

Tarqiyyah (lit. 'ascension'): the education of the youth through study and research, and through the idea of future leadership (*hizbut*). This focuses on the eligibility of the successor based on their spiritual qualities and leadership competence, rather than on *silsila-baraka*.

Tasawwuf: Sufism or esotericism.

Tijaniyya: Sufi order founded by Ahmed al-Tijani (1737–1815), who claimed a direct link with the Prophet (and thus his order too, *al-tariqa al-Muhammadyya*). He asserted his supremacy over other Sufi saints, as Mohammed had over other prophets, and he made the repudiation of other *taruq* the condition for initiation into his own *tariqa*.

Ulema (sing. Ālim; lit. 'scholar'): Muslim scholarly arbiters of Sharia law, often versed in legal jurisprudence (*fiqh*). They were appointed by the khalifs to represent the spiritual knowledge of the Muslim State.

Ummah: the worldwide Islamic community.

Wahabi: a movement founded by Mohammed Abd al-Wahhab (1703–92) in Arabia. It promoted religious revival as strict adherence to the teachings of Islam based on the Qur'an and the Hadiths, without resorting to their allegorical interpretation. From the beginning of the twentieth century, Egyptian *ulema* of the Wahabiyya school became fierce opponents of the Sufi *turuq* and resented the latter's popularity.

(Al-)zakāt: the annual tithe required of Muslims. This is one of the five Pillars of Islam, together with *al-shahada* (declaration of faith), *al-hadji* (pilgrimage to Mecca), *al-salat* (prayer) and *al-ramadan* (ritual fasting during the lunar month of Ramadan).

References

Abun-Nasr, Jamil M. 2007. *Muslim Communities of Grace: The Sufi Brotherhoods in Islamic Religious Life*. London: Hurst.

Accoroni, Dafne. 2018. 'Du Monde Francophone aux *Francophonies* des Migrants: l'Équation d'un Héritage en Transformation et Spécificité des Migrations Ouest Africaines', *Revue Internationale des Francophonies* 4. Retrieved from https://dx .doi.org/10.35562/rif.730.

Agier, Michel. 2011. *Managing the Undesirable: Refugee Camps and Humanitarian Government*. Cambridge: Polity Press.

Ahmed, Akbar. 2018. *Journey into Europe: Islam, Immigration, and Identity.* Washington, DC: Brookings Institution Press.

Ali-Bencherif, Mohammed-Zakaria and Azzeddine Mahieddinne. 2019. 'La Mobilité Universitaire des Étudiants Algériens en France: De la Mise en Discours des Pays d'Origine et d'Accueil', in Nathalie Thamin and Mohamed-Zakaria Ali-Bencherif (eds), *Mobilités dans l'Espace Migratoire Algérie-France-Canada*. Aix-en-Provence: Presses Universitaires de Provence, pp. 97–111.

Babou, Cheick Anta. 2003. 'Educating the Murid: Theory and Practices of Education in Amadu Bamba's Thought', *Journal of Religion in Africa* 33: 310–27.

———. 2007. *Fighting the Greater Jihad: Amadou Bamba and the Founding of the Mouridiyya of Senegal, 1853–1913*. Athens, OH: Ohio University Press.

Barley, Nigel. 1986. *A Plague of Caterpillars: A Return to the African Bush*. New York: Viking.

Barou, Jacques. 2002. 'Les Immigrations Africaines en France au Tournant du Siècle', *Homme & Migrations* 1239: 6–18.

Bateson, Gregory. 1935. 'Culture Contact and Schismogenesis', *Man* 35: 178–83.

Bava, Sophie. 2010. 'Religions Transnationales et Migrations: Regards Croisés sur un Champ en Mouvement', *Autrepart* 4(56): 3–15.

————. 2004. 'Le Dahira Urbain: Lieu de Pouvoir du Mouridisme', *Les Annales de la Recherche Urbaine* 96: 135–43.

Bazin, Laurent, Robert Gibb, Catherine Neveu and Monique Selim. 2006. 'The Broken Myth: Popular Unrest and the "Republican Model of Integration" in France', *Anthropology Today* 22(2): 16–17.

Beauchemin, Cris, Christelle Hamel and Simon Patrick (eds). 2016. *Trajectoires et Origines: Enquête sur la Diversité des Populations en France*. Paris: INED.

Belguidoum, Saïd, and Sidi Mohammed Mohammedi. 2015. 'Les Migrations – Vues du Sud', *Insaniyat, Algerian Journal of Anthropology and Social Sciences* 69–70: 11–23.

Beneduce, Roberto. 2002. *Trance e Possessione in Africa: Corpi, Mimesi, Storia*. Turin: Bollati Boringhieri.

Boas, Franz. 1920. 'The Methods of Ethnology', *American Anthropologist* 22(4): 311–21.

Brenner, Emmanuel (ed.). 2002. *Les Territoires Perdus de la Republique: Anti-Semitism, Racisme et Sexisme en Milieu Scolaire*. Paris: Éditions Mille et Une Nuit.

Brenner, Louis. 1985. *Réflexions sur le Savoir Islamique en Afrique de l'Ouest*. Talence: France.

Brunet, Laurence. 2010. 'La Réception en Droit Français des Institutions Familiales de Droit Musulman: Vertus et Faiblesses d'un Compromise', *Droit et Cultures* 59: 231–51.

Carter, Donald Martin. 1997. *States of Grace: Senegalese in Italy and the New European Immigration*. Minneapolis, MN: Minnesota University Press.

Clifford, James. 1992. 'Travelling Cultures', in Lawrence Grossberg, Cary Nelson, and Paula Treichler (eds), *Cultural Studies*. New York: Routledge, pp. 96–116.

Coe, Cati. 2011. 'What is Love? The Materiality of Care in Ghanaian Transnational Families', *International Migration* 49(6): 7–24.

Cole, Jennifer, and Christian Groes (eds). 2016. *Affective Circuits: African Migrations to Europe and the Pursuit of Social Regeneration*. Chicago: University of Chicago Press.

Collignon, René. 2004. 'Émergence de la Psychiatrie Transculturelle au Lendemain de la Seconde Guerre Mondiale (Références Africaines)', in Marie-Rose Moro, Quitterie de la Noë and Yoram Mouchnick (eds), *Manuelle de Psychiatrie Transculturelle: Travaille Clinique, Travaille Sociale*. Grenoble: La Pensée Sauvage, pp. 79–107.

Collomb, Henri. 1979. 'De l'Ethnopsychiatrie à la Psychiatrie Sociale', *Revue Canadienne de Psychiatrie* 24: 459–69.

————. 1980. 'Pour une Psychiatrie Sociale', *Thérapie Familiale* 1(2): 99–107.

Copans, Jean. 1980. *Les Marabouts de l'Arachide: La Confrérie Mouride et les Paysans du Sénégal*. Paris. Le Sycomore.

Coppolani, Xavier, and Octave Depont. 1897. *Les Confréries Religieuses Musulmanes*. Paris: Jourdan.

Corin, Ellen, Gilles Bibeau and Elisabeth Uchôa. 1993. 'Éléments d'une Sémiologie Anthropologique des Troubles Psychiques chez les Bambara, Soninké et Bwa du Mali', *Anthropologie et Sociétés* 17(1–2): 125–56.

Coulon, Christian. 1981. *Le Marabout et le Prince: Islam et Pouvoir au Sénégal*. Paris: Pedone.

Cruise O'Brien, Donal B. 1971. *The Murid of Senegal: The Political and Economic Organization of an Islamic Brotherhood*. Oxford: Clarendon Press.

———. 1988. 'Charisma Comes to Town: Mouride Urbanization, 1945–1986', in Donal B. Cruise O'Brien and Christian Coulon (eds), *Charisma and Brotherhood in African Islam*. Oxford: Clarendon Press, pp. 135–55.

———. 2003. *Symbolic Confrontations: Muslims Imagining the State in Africa*. London: Hurst.

De Bruijn, Mirjam, Han Van Dijk and Rijk Van Dijk. 2001. 'Cultures of Travel: Fulbe Pastoralists in Central Mali and Pentecostalism in Ghana', in Mirjam de Bruijn, Rijk Van Dijk and Dick Foeken (eds), *Mobile Africa: Changing Patterns of Movement in Africa and Beyond*. Leiden: Brill, pp. 63–88.

Devereux, George. 1978. *Ethnopsychoanalysis: Psychoanalysis and Anthropology as Complementary Frames of Reference*. Berkeley, CA: University of California Press.

———. 1980. *Basic Problems of Ethnopsychiatry*. Chicago: University of Chicago Press.

Diop, Moustapha. 1993. 'L'Immigration Oust-Africaine en Europe', *Revue* Études *Internationales* 24(1): 111–24.

———. 2000. 'Le Mouvement Associatif Islamique en France', *Croire Aujourd'hui* 98: 23–26.

Diop, Moustapha, and Laurence Michalak. 1996. '"Refuge" and "Prison": Islam, Ethnicity and the Adaptation of Space in Workers' Housing in France', in Metcalf B. Daly (ed.), *Making Muslim Space in North America and Europe*. Berkeley, CA: University of California Press, pp. 74–91.

Diouf, Mamadou. 2000. 'The Senegalese Mouride Trade Diaspora and the Making of a Vernacular Cosmopolitanism', *Public Culture* 12(3): 679–702.

Dorris, Alexa K. 2011. 'Soul Medicine: The Role of Traditional Senegalese Music in a Therapeutic Context'. *Independent Study Project (ISP) Collection*. Retrieved 22 March 2022 from https://digitalcollections.sit.edu/isp_collection/1010.

Douglas, Mary. 2002 [1966]. *Purity and Danger: An Analysis of Concepts of Pollution and Taboo*. London: Routledge.

Duriez, Julien. n.d. '"À Bara, on est comme des Animaux": À Montreuil, les Travailleurs Etrangers du Foyer Bara Espèrent un Logement Digne'. *La Croix*. Retrieved 22 March 2022 from https://services.la-croix.com/webdocs/pages/longform_foyer_migrants/index.html.

Ebin, Victoria. 1992. 'A la Recherche de Nouveaux Poissons: Stratégies Commerciales Mourides en Temps de Crise', *Politique Africaine* 45: 86–99.

———. 1996. 'Making Room Versus Creating Space: The Construction of Special Categories by Itinerant Mourid Traders', in Metcalf B. Daly (ed.), *Making Muslim Space in North America and Europe*. Berkeley, CA: University of California Press, pp. 92–109.

Evans-Pritchard, Edward Evan. 1937. *Witchcraft, Oracles and Magic among the Azande*. Oxford: Clarendon Press.

Extramiana, Claire, and Piet Van Avermaet. 2010. 'Apprendre la Langue du Pays d'Accueil', *Hommes et Migrations* 1288: 8–20.

Fábos, Anita H. 2008. *Brothers or Others? Propriety and Gender for Muslim Arab Sudanese in Egypt.* New York: Berghahn Books.

Fall, Mar. 2005. *Le Destin des Africains Noirs en France: Discriminations, Assimilation, Repli Communautaire.* Paris: Harmattan.

Fanon, Frantz. 1963 [1961]. *The Wretched of the Earth.* London: Macgibbon & Kee.

———. 1967 [1952]. *Black Skins, White Masks.* Harmondsworth: Penguin.

Fassin, Didier. 1992. *Pouvoir et Maladie en Afrique: Anthropologie Sociale dans la Banlieue de Dakar.* Paris: PUF.

———. 1999. 'L'Ethnopsychiatrie et ses Réseaux: L'Influence qui Grandit', *Genèses* 35(35): 146–71.

———. 2000. 'Les Politiques de l'Ethnopsychiatrie: La Psyché Africaine, des Colonies Britanniques aux Banlieues Parisiennes', *L'Homme* 153: 231–50.

———. 2009. 'Le Droit d'Avoir des Droits', *Hommes et Migrations. Santé et Droits des Étrangers: Realités et Énjeux* 1282: 20–23.

Feldman-Savelsberg, Pamela. 2016. *Mothers on the Move: Reproducing Belonging between Africa and Europe.* Chicago: University of Chicago Press.

Fievet, Michel. 1999. *Le Livre Blanc des Travailleurs Immigrés des Foyers: Du Non-Droit au Droit.* Paris: Ciemi.

Foucault, Michel. 1986 [1967 Lecture Notes]. 'Of Other Spaces', *Diacritics* 16(1): 22–27.

Frégosi, Franck. 2005. 'Les Enjeux Liés à la Structuration de l'Islam en France', in Rémy Leveau and KhadijaMohsen-Finan (eds), *Musulmans de France et d'Europe.* Paris: CNRS Éditions, pp. 99–114.

Friedlander, Shems, Muzaffer Ozak and Hamid Amidi. 1978. *Ninety-Nine Names of Allah: The Beautiful Names.* London: Wildwood House.

Gellner, Ernest. 1992. *Postmodernism, Reason and Religion.* London. Routledge.

Geschiere, Peter. 2005. 'Funerals and Belonging: Different Patterns in South Cameroon', *African Studies Review* 48(2): 45–64.

Geschiere, Peter, and Josef Gugler. 1998. 'The Urban-Rural Connection: Changing Issues of Belonging and Identification', *Africa: Journal of the International African Institute* 68(3): 309–19.

Gilroy, Paul. 1992 [1987]. *There Ain't No Black in the Union Jack.* London: Routledge.

Gilsenan, Michael. 1973. *Saint and Sufi in Modern Egypt: An Essay in the Sociology of Religion.* Oxford: Clarendon Press.

Glover, John. 2007. *Sufism and Jihad in Modern Senegal: The Murid Order.* Rochester, NY: University of Rochester Press.

Gnisci, Donata, and Marie Trémolières. 2006. 'Overview of International Migration from the Global to the African Level', *Frontières et Intégrations en Afrique de l'Ouest: Cross-Border Diaries* 4: 9–13.

Gounongbé, Ari. 2009. 'Migration, Pathologie du Retour et Prévention', *Transfaire & Culture* 1: 27–36.

Grillo, Ralph, and Bruno Riccio. 2004. 'Translocal Development: Italy-Senegal', *Population, Space and Place* 10(2): 99–111.

Gugler, Josef. 2002. 'The Son of the Hawk Does Not Remain Abroad: The Urban-Rural Connection in Africa', *African Studies Review* 45(1): 21–41.

Gupta, Akhil, and James Ferguson (eds). 1997. *Anthropological Locations: Boundaries and Grounds of a Field Science*. Berkeley, CA: University of California Press.

Habermas, Jürgen. 1991. *The Structural Transformation of the Public Sphere: An Inquiry into a Category of Bourgeois Society*. Cambridge, MA: MIT Press.

Hannaford, Dinah. 2017. *Marriage without Borders: Transnational Spouses in Neoliberal Senegal*. Philadelphia, PA: University of Pennsylvania Press.

Hefner, Robert W. 1998. 'Multiple Modernities: Christianity, Islam, and Hinduism in a Globalizing Age', *Annual Review of Anthropology* 27: 83–104.

Huntington, Samuel P. 1996. *The Clash of Civilizations*. New York: Simon & Schuster.

Jamous, Raymond. 1981. *Honneur et Baraka: Les Structures Sociales Traditionnelles dans le Rif*. Paris: Maison des Sciences de l'Homme.

Kante, Nambala. 1993. *Forgerons d'Afrique Noire: Transmission des Savoirs Traditionnels en Pays Malinké*. Paris: Harmattan.

Kareem, Jafar, and Roland Littlewood (eds). 2000 [1992]. *Intercultural Therapy*. London: Blackwell Science.

Kastoryano, Riva. 2006. 'France's Headscarf Affair', in Tariq Modood, Anna Traindafyllidou and Ricard Zapata-Barrero (eds), *Multiculturalism, Muslims and Citizenship*. London: Routledge, pp. 57–69.

Keller, Richard C. 2007. *Colonial Madness: Psychiatry in French North Africa*. Chicago: University of Chicago Press.

Khalifa, Najat. 2005. 'Possession and Jinn', *Journal of the Royal Society of Medicine* 98(8): 351–53.

Kleinman, Arthur. 1980. *Patients and Healers in the Context of Culture: An Exploration of the Borderland between Anthropology, Medicine, and Psychiatry*. Berkeley, CA: University of California Press.

———. 1988. *The Illness Narratives: Suffering, Healing, and the Human Condition*. New York: Basic Books.

Kleinman, Julie. 2019. *Adventure Capital: Migration and the Making of an African Hub in Paris*. Berkeley, CA: University of California Press.

Könönen, Jukka. 2021. 'The Absent Presence of the Deportation Apparatus: Methodological Challenges in the Production of Knowledge on Immigration Detention', *Social Anthropology* 29(3): 619–34.

Kothari, Uma. 2008. 'Global Peddlers and Local Networks: Migrant Cosmopolitanisms', *Environment and Planning D: Society and Space*, 26(3): 500-516.

Kuczynski, Liliane. 1988. 'Return of Love: Everyday Life and African Divination in Paris', *Anthropology Today* 4(3): 6–9.

———. 2002. *Les Marabouts Africains à Paris*. Paris: CNRS Éditions.

———. 2004. 'Chiffres, Lettres et Prières: L'Islam des Marabouts Africains à Paris', in Y-C Zarka (ed.), *L'Islam en France*. Paris: PUF, pp. 547–52.

Lambek, Michael. 1981. *Human Spirits: A Cultural Account of Trance in Mayotte*. Cambridge: Cambridge University Press.

Laplantine, François, and Alexis Nouss. 2011 [1997]. *Le Métissage: Un Exposé pour Comprendre, Un Essai pour Réfléchir*. Paris: Téraèdre.

Last, Murray. 1981. 'The Importance of Knowing about Not Knowing', *Social Science & Medicine* 15(3): 387–92.

———. 1988. 'Charisma and Medicine in Northern Nigeria', in Christian Coulon and Donal B. Cruise O'Brien (eds), *Charisma and Brotherhood in African Islam*. Oxford: Caledonian Press, pp. 183–204.

———. 2007. 'The Importance of Knowing about Not Knowing', in Roland Littlewood (ed.), *On Knowing and Not Knowing in the Anthropology of Medicine*. Walnut Creek, CA: Left Coast Press, pp. 1–17.

Laurence, Jonathan, and Justin Vaïsse. 2006. *Integrating Islam: Political and Religious Challenges in Contemporary France*. Washington, DC: Brookings Institution Press.

Lavigne Delville, Philippe. 1991. *La Rizière et la Valise: Irrigation, Migration et Stratégies Paysannes dans la Vallée du Fleuve Sénégal*. Paris: Syros-Alternatives.

Leclerc, Jean-Marc. 2018. 'Immigration Clandestine: La Seine-Saint-Denis Débordée', *Le Figaro*, 4 July. Retrieved 22 March 2022 from https://www.lefigaro.fr/actualite-france/2018/07/04/01016-20180704ARTFIG00238-en-seine-saint-denis-l-etat-desempare-face-a-l-ampleur-du-nombre-de-clandestins.php.

Lessault, David, and Cris Beauchemin. 2009. 'Les Migrations d'Afrique Subsaharienne en Europe: Un Essor encore Limité', *Population & Sociétés* 452: 1–4.

Lévi-Strauss, Claude. 1949. *Les Structures Élémentaires de la Parenté*. Paris: PUF.

Littlewood, Roland. 1989. 'Science, Shamanism and Hermeneutics. Recent Writing on Psychoanalysis', *Anthropology Today* 5(1): 5–11.

———. 1991. 'Against Pathology: The New Psychiatry and its Critics', *British Journal of Psychiatry* 159: 696–702.

———. 1995. 'Psychopathology and Personal Agency: Modernity, Culture Change and Eating Disorders in South Asian Societies', *British Journal of Medical Psychology* 68(1): 45–63.

———. 2003. 'Why Narrative? Why Now?', *Anthropology & Medicine* 10(2): 255–61.

Littlewood, Roland and Maurice Lipsedge. (III ed. 2004) [1982]. *Aliens and Alienists: Ethnic Minorities and Psychiatry*. London: Routledge.

Malinowski, Bronisław. 1922. *Argonauts of the Western Pacific: An Account of Native Enterprise and Adventure in the Archipelagos of Melanesian New Guinea*. London: Routledge.

Manchuelle, François. 1997. *Willing Migrants: Soninké Labour Diasporas, 1848–1960*. London: James Currey.

Mann, Gregory. 2003. 'Immigrants and Arguments in France and West Africa', *Comparative Studies in Society and History* 45(2): 362–85.

Marty, Paul. 1917. *Études sur l'Islam au Sénégal*, vol. 2. Paris: Leroux.

Massing, Andreas W. 2000. 'The Wangara, an Old Soninke Diaspora in West Africa?', *Cahiers d'Etudes Africaines*, 40(158): 281-308.

Mauss, Marcel. 2002 [1966]. *The Gift: Form and Reason for Exchange in Archaic Societies*. London: Routledge.

Mayanthi, L. Fernando. 2014. *The Republic Unsettled: Muslim French and the Contradictions of Secularism*. Durham, NC: Duke University Press.

Mead, Margaret. 2016 [1977]. *Letters from the Field, 1925–1975*. New York: HarperCollins.

Miller, Thaddeus R., Timothy D. Baird, Caitlin M. Littlefield, Gary Kofinas, F. Stuart Chapin III and Charles L. Redman. 2008. 'Epistemological Pluralism:

Reorganizing Interdisciplinary Research', *Ecology and Society* 13(2). Retrieved 22 March 2022 from http://www.ecologyandsociety.org/vol13/iss2/art46.

Migrations et Santé. 2003. *Diagnostique Médico-Social: Foyer AFTAM Montreuil (93)*. Paris: PRAPS.

Modood, Tariq. 2006. 'British Muslims and the Politics of Multiculturalism', in Tariq Modood, Anna Triandafyllidou and Ricar Zapata-Barrero (eds), *Multiculturalism, Muslims and Citizenship*. London: Routledge, pp. 37–56.

Mohammedi, Sidi Mohammed (ed.). 2014. *Abdelmalek Sayad: Migrations et Mondialisation*. Oran: CRASC.

Moro, Marie Rose. 2002. *Enfants d'Ici Venus d'Ailleurs: Naître et Grandir en France*. Paris: La Découverte.

Moro, Marie Rose, Quitterie De la Noë and Yoram Mouchenik. 2006. *Manuel de Psychiatrie Transculturelle*. Grenoble: La Pensée Sauvage.

Nathan, Tobie. 1986. *La Folie des Autres: Traité d'Ethnopsychiatrie Clinique*. Paris: Dunod.

———. 1994. *L'Influence qui Guérit*. Paris: Editions Odile Jacob.

Noiriel, Gérard. 1988. *Le Creuset Français: Histoire de l'Immigration, XIXe–XXe Siècle*. Paris: Seuil.

Ortigues, Marie-Cécile, and Edmond Ortigues. 1984. *Œdipe Africaine*. Paris: Harmattan.

Orwell, George. 1989 [1937]. *The Road to Wigan Pier*. London: Penguin.

Park, Robert E., and Ernest W. Burgess. 1921. *Introduction to the Science of Sociology*. Chicago: University of Chicago Press.

Pécoud, Antoine. 2004. 'German-Turkish Entrepreneurship and the Economic Dimension of Multiculturalism', in Han Entzinger, Marco Martiniello and Catherine Wihtol de Wenden (eds), *Migration between States and Markets*. Aldershot: Ashgate, pp. 119–29.

Piga, Adriana. 2002. *Dakar et les Ordres Soufis: Processus Socioculturels et Développement Urbain au Sénégal Contemporain*. Paris: Harmattan.

Pitt-Rivers, Julian. 1992. 'Postscript: The Place of Grace in Anthropology', in John George Peristiany and Julian Pitt-Rivers (eds), *Honour and Grace in Anthropology*. Cambridge: Cambridge University Press, pp. 215–46.

Pollet, Eric, and Grace Winter. 1971. *La Société Soninké (Dyahunu, Mali)*. Bruxelles: Université Libre de Bruxelles.

Popenoe, Rebecca. 2003. *Feeding Desire: Fatness and Beauty in the Sahara*. London: Routledge.

Portes, Alejandro. 1995. *The Economic Sociology of Immigration: Essays on Networks, Ethnicity and Entrepreneurship*. New York: Russell Sage Foundation.

Portes, Alejandro, and Julia Sensenbrenner. 1993. 'Embeddedness and Immigration: Notes on the Social Determinants of Economic Action', *American Journal of Sociology* 98(6): 1320–50.

Portes, Alejandro, and Min Zhou. 1993. 'The New Second Generation: Segmented Assimilation and its Variants', *The Annals of the American Academy of Political and Social Sciences* 530: 74–98.

Portes, Alejandro, and Jozsef Borocz. 1989. 'Contemporary Immigration: Theoretical Perspectives on its Determinants and Modes of Incorporation', *International Migration Review* 23(3): 606–30.

Quiminal, Catherine. 1990. 'Du Foyer au Village: L'Initiative Retrouvée', *Homme et Migrations* 1131: 19–24.

———. 1991. *Gens d'Ici, Gens d'Ailleurs*. Paris: Christian Burgois.

———. 2002. 'Retours Contraints, Retours Construits des Émigrés Maliens', *Hommes et Migrations: Retours d'en France* 1236: 35–43.

Quiminal, Catherine, and Mahamet Timera. 2002. '1974–2002, Les Mutations de l'Immigration Ouest-Africaine', *Hommes et Migrations: Africains, Citoyens d'Ici et de Là-bas* 1239: 19–32.

Rhazzali, Mohammed Khalid. 2015. *Comunicazione Interculturale e Sfera Pubblica: Diversità e Mediazione nelle Istituzioni*. Rome: Carocci Editore.

Riccio, Bruno. 2001. 'From "Ethnic Group" to "Transnational Community"? Senegalese Migrants' Ambivalent Experiences and Multiple Trajectories', *Journal of Ethnic and Migration Studies* 27(4): 583–99.

———. 2003. 'More Than a Trading Diaspora: Senegalese Transnational Experiences in Emilia Romagna (Italy)', in Khalid Koser (ed.), *New African Diasporas*. London: Routledge, pp. 273–84.

Rivers, William Halse Rivers. 1923. *Conflict and Dream*. London: Kegan Paul, Trench and Trubner.

Robinson, David. 2000a. *Paths of Accommodation: Muslim Societies and French Colonial Authorities in Senegal and Mauritania, 1880–1920*. Oxford: James Currey.

———. 2000b. '"French Africans" – Faidherbe, Archinard and Coppolani: The "Creators" of Senegal, Soudan and Mauritania', in R. James Bingen, David Robinson and John M. Staatz (eds), *Democracy and Development in Mali*. East Lansing, MI: Michigan State University Press, pp. 23–40.

Robinson, David, and Jean-Louis Triaud (eds). 1997. *Le Temps des Marabouts: Itinéraires et Stratégies Islamiques en Afrique Occidentale Française v. 1880–1960*. Paris: Karthala.

Rosenberg, Clifford D. 2006. *Policing Paris: the Origins of Modern Immigration Control between the Wars*. London: Cornell University Press.

Safi, Mirna. 2006. 'Le Processus d'Intégration des Immigrés en France: Inégalités et Segmentation', *Revue Française de Sociologie* 47(1) :3-48.

Saraiva, Clara. 2008. 'Transnational Migrants and Transnational Spirits: An African Religion in Lisbon', *Journal of Ethnic and Migration Studies* 34(2): 253–69.

Sargent, Carolyn Fishel. 2006. 'Reproductive Strategies in Islamic Discourse', *Medical Anthropology Quarterly* 20(1): 31–49.

Sargent, Carolyn Fishel and Larchanché Stéphanie. 2009a. 'The Construction of "Cultural Difference" and its Therapeutic Significance in Immigrant Mental Health Services in France', *Culture, Medicine and Psychiatry* 33(1): 2–20.

———. 2009b. 'Sur les Pas de l'Anthropologie Médicale Clinique en France: La Maturation d'un Approche sur la Place de la Culture dans les Soins de Santé Mentale', *Transfaire et Culture* 1: 100-107.

Sarr, Papa Amadou. 2009. 'Transfert de Fonds des Migrants et Développement en Afrique: Une Étude de Cas sur le Sénégal', *Techniques Financières et Développement*: 15–27.

Sayad, Abdelmalek. 1979. 'Les Enfants Illégitimes', *Actes de la Recherche en Sciences Sociales* 26(26–27): 117–132.

———. 1994. 'Qu'est-ce que l'Intégration?', *Hommes & Migrations* 1182: 8–14.

———. 1998. 'Le Retour, Élément Constitutif de la Condition de l'Immigré', *Migrations Société* 10(57): 9–45.

———. 1999. *La Double Absence: Des Illusions de l'Émigré aux Souffrances de l'Immigré*. Paris: Le Seuil.

Schmidt di Friedberg, Ottavia. 1994. *Islam, Solidarietà e Lavoro: I Muridi Senegalesi in Italia*. Turin: Fondazione G. Agnelli.

Schönwälder, Karen, Sören Petermann, Jörg Hüttermann, Steven Vertovec, Miles Hewstone, Dietlind Stolle, Katharina Schmid and Thomas Schmitt. 2016. *Diversity and Contact: Immigration and Social Interaction in German Cities*. Basingstoke: Palgrave Macmillan.

Shipton, Parker. 2007. *The Nature of Entrustment: Intimacy, Exchange, and the Sacred in Africa*. New Haven, CT: Yale University Press.

———. 2010. *Credit between Cultures: Farmers, Financiers, and Misunderstanding in Africa*. New Haven, CT: Yale University Press.

Sow, Alfâ Ibrâhîm. 1980. *Anthropological Structures of Madness in Black Africa*. New York: International Universities Press.

Stoller, Paul. 1989. *Fusion of the Worlds: An Ethnology of Possession among the Songhay of Niger*. Chicago: University of Chicago Press.

———. 1995. *Embodying Colonial Memories: Spirit Possession, Power, and the Hauka in West Africa*. London: Routledge.

Strathern, Marilyn. 1987. *Dealing with Inequality: Analysing Gender Relations in Melanesia and Beyond*. Cambridge: Cambridge University Press.

———. 2004. [1991]. *Partial Connections*. Walnut Creek, CA: AltaMira Press.

———. 2016. *Before and After Gender: Sexual Mythologies of Everyday Life*. Chicago: Hau.

Sylla, Aïda, Omar Ndoye and Momar Gueye. 2001. 'Importance du Contexte Socioculturel dans la Psychopathie en Afrique: Une Observation Clinique', *L'Évolution Psychiatrique* 66(4): 647–54.

Taneja, Anand Vivek. 2018. *Jennealogy: Time, Islam and Ecological Thought in the Medieval Ruins of Delhi*. Stanford, CA: Stanford University Press.

Tetreault, Chantal. 2015. *Transcultural Teens: Performing Youth Identities in French Cités*. Hoboken, NJ: John Wiley & Sons.

Timera, Mahamet. 1996. *Les Soninké en France: D'une Histoire à L'autre*. Paris: Karthala.

Traoré, Alioune. 1983. *Cheikh Hamahoullah, Homme de Foi et Résistant: Islam et Colonisation en Afrique*. Paris: Maisonneuve et Laros.

Trauner, Helen. 2005. 'Dimensions of West African Immigration to France: Malian Immigrant Women in Paris', *Stichproben: Wiener Zeitschrift fur kritische Afrikastudien* 8(5): 221–35.

Tribalat, Michèle. 1995. *Faire France: Une Grande Enquête sur les Immigrés et leurs Enfants*. Paris: La Découverte.

———. 1996. *De l'Immigration à l'Assimilation: Enquête sur les Populations d'Origine Ètrangère en France*. Paris: La Découverte.

Trovão, Susana. 2014. 'Comparing Transnational and Local Influences on Immigrant Transnational Families of African and Asian Origin in Portugal', *Journal of Family Issues* 37(14): 2045–69.

Turner, Colin. 1996. *The Ubiquitous Faqih: A Reconsideration of the Terms Iman, Islam and 'Ilm and their Role in the Rise to Predominance of the Jurist in the Islamic World of Learning*. Durham, NC: University of Durham Press.

Varlik, Nükhet. 2017. *Plague and Contagion in the Islamic Mediterranean: New Histories of Disease in Ottoman Society*. Kalamazoo, MI: Arc Humanities Press.

Vertovec, Steven. 2007. 'Super-Diversity and its Implications', *Ethnic and Racial Studies* 29(6): 1024–54.

———. 2019. 'Talking around Super-Diversity', *Ethnic and Racial Studies* 42(1): 125–39.

Weil, Patrick. 2008. *How to be French: Nationality in the Making since 1789*. Durham, NC: Duke University Press.

Werbner, Pnina. 2003. *Pilgrims of Love: The Anthropology of a Global Sufi Cult*. London: Hurst.

———. 2004. 'The Predicament of Diaspora and Millennial Islam: Reflections on September 11', *Ethnicities* 4(4): 451–76.

———. 2008. 'The Cosmopolitan Encounter: Social Anthropology and the Kindness of Strangers', in Pnina Werbner (ed.), *Anthropology and the New Cosmopolitanism: Rooted, Feminist and Vernacular Perspectives*. Oxford: Berg, pp. 47–68.

Werbner, Pnina, and Helen Basu. 1998. 'The Embodiment of Charisma', in Pnina Werbner and Helen Basu (eds), *Embodying Charisma: Modernity, Locality and the Performance of Emotion in Sufi Cults*. London: Routledge, pp. 3–27.

Wihtol de Wenden, Catherine. 1998. 'Young Muslim Women in France: Cultural and Psychological Adjustments', *Political Psychology* 19(1): 133–46.

———. 2001. 'Un Essai de Typologie des Nouvelles Mobilités', *Hommes et Migrations* 1233: 5–12.

———. 2005. 'Seconde Generation: Le Cas Français', in Rémy Leveau and Khadija Mohsen-Finan (eds), *Musulmans de France et d'Europe*. Paris: CNRS Éditions, pp. 1–19.

———. 2016. *Migrations: Une Nouvelle Donne*. Paris: Maison des Sciences de l'Homme.

Yount-André, Chelsie. 2020. 'Strategic Investments in Multiple Middle Classes: Morals and Mobility between Paris and Dakar', *Africa Today* 66(3–4): 89–112.

Zehraoui, Ahsène. 1996. 'Processus Différentiels d'Intégration au Sein des Familles Algériennes en France', *Revue Française de Sociologie* 37(2): 237–61.

Zempleni, Andras. 1966. 'La Dimension Thérapeutique du Culte du Rab: Ndöp, Tuuru et Samp. Rites de Possession chez les Lebou et les Wolof', *Psychopathologie Africaine* 2(3): 295–439.

Zobel, Clemens. 1996. 'Les Génies du Kòma: Identités Locales, Logiques Religieuses et Enjeux Socio-Politiques dans les Monts Manding du Mali', *Cahiers d'Études Africaines, Mélanges Maliens* 36(144): 625–58.

'Zoom'. 2021. *La CGT Ensemble* 143: 2.

Index

Lightning Source UK Ltd.
Milton Keynes UK
UKHW021140080922
408480UK00003B/362